Life of Robert Burns

Allan Cunningham

ISBN-13:
978-1500475581

ISBN-10:
1500475580

Life of Robert Burns.

Robert Burns, the chief of the peasant poets of Scotland, was born in a little mud-walled cottage on the banks of Doon, near "Alloway's auld haunted kirk," in the shire of Ayr, on the 25th day of January, 1759. As a natural mark of the event, a sudden storm at the same moment swept the land: the gabel-wall of the frail dwelling gave way, and the babe-bard was hurried through a tempest of wind and sleet to the shelter of a securer hovel. He was the eldest born of three sons and three daughters; his father, William, who in his native Kincardineshire wrote his name Burness, was bred a gardener, and sought for work in the West; but coming from the lands of the noble family of the Keiths, a suspicion accompanied him that he had been out — as rebellion was softly called — in the forty-five: a suspicion fatal to his hopes of rest and bread, in so loyal a district; and it was only when the clergyman of his native parish certified his loyalty that he was permitted to toil. This suspicion of Jacobitism, revived by Burns himself, when he rose into fame, seems not to have influenced either the feelings, or the tastes of Agnes Brown, a young woman on the Doon, whom he wooed and married in December, 1757, when he was thirty-six years old. To support her, he leased a small piece of ground, which he converted into a nursery and garden, and to shelter her, he raised with his own hands that humble abode where she gave birth to her eldest son.

The elder Burns was a well-informed, silent, austere man, who endured no idle gaiety, nor indecorous language: while he relaxed somewhat the hard, stern creed of the Covenanting times, he enforced all the work-day, as well as sabbath-day observances, which the Calvinistic kirk requires, and scrupled at promiscuous dancing, as the staid of our own day scruple at the waltz. His wife was of a milder mood: she was blest with a singular fortitude of temper; was as devout of heart, as she was calm of mind; and loved, while busied in her household concerns, to sweeten the bitterer moments of life, by chanting the songs and ballads of her country, of which her store was great. The garden and nursery prospered so much, that he was induced to widen his views, and by the help of his kind landlord, the laird of Doonholm, and the more questionable aid of borrowed money, he entered upon a neighbouring farm, named Mount Oliphant, extending to an hundred acres. This was in 1765; but the land was hungry and sterile; the seasons proved rainy and rough; the toil was certain, the reward unsure; when to his sorrow, the laird of Doonholm — a generous Ferguson — died: the strict terms of the lease, as well as the rent, were exacted by a harsh factor, and with his wife and children, he was obliged, after a losing struggle of six years, to relinquish the farm, and seek shelter on the grounds of Lochlea, some ten miles off, in the parish of Tarbolton. When, in after-days, men's characters were in the hands of his eldest son, the scoundrel factor sat for that lasting portrait of insolence and wrong, in the "Twa Dogs."

In this new farm William Burns seemed to strike root, and thrive. He was strong of body and ardent of mind: every day brought increase of vigour to his three sons, who, though very young, already put their hands to the plough, the reap-hook, and the flail. But it seemed that nothing which he undertook was decreed in the end to prosper: after four seasons of prosperity a change ensued: the farm was far from cheap; the gains under any lease were then so little, that the loss of a few pounds was ruinous to a farmer: bad seed and wet seasons had their usual influence: "The gloom of hermits and the moil of galley-slaves," as the poet, alluding to those days, said, were endured to no purpose; when, to crown all, a difference arose between the landlord and the tenant, as to the terms of the lease; and the early days of the poet, and the declining years of his father, were harassed by disputes, in which sensitive minds are sure to suffer.

Amid these labours and disputes, the poet's father remembered the worth of religious and moral instruction: he took part of this upon himself. A week-day in Lochlea wore the sober looks of a Sunday: he read the Bible and explained, as intelligent peasants are accustomed to do, the sense, when dark or difficult; he loved to discuss the spiritual meanings, and gaze on the mystical splendours of the Revelations. He was aided in these labours, first, by the schoolmaster of Alloway-mill, near the Doon; secondly, by John Murdoch, student of divinity, who undertook to teach arithmetic, grammar, French, and Latin, to the boys of Lochlea, and the sons of five neighboring farmers. Murdoch, who was an enthusiast in learning, much of a pedant, and such a judge of genius that he thought wit should always be laughing, and poetry wear an eternal smile, performed his task well: he found Robert to be quick in apprehension, and not afraid to study when knowledge was the reward. He taught him to turn verse into its natural prose order; to supply all the ellipses, and not to desist till the sense was clear and plain: he also, in their walks, told him the names of different objects both in Latin and French; and though his knowledge of these languages never amounted to much, he approached the grammar of the English tongue, through the former, which was of material use to him, in his poetic compositions. Burns was, even in those early days, a sort of enthusiast in all that concerned the glory of Scotland; he used to fancy himself a soldier of the days of the Wallace and the Bruce: loved to strut after the bag-pipe and the drum, and read of the bloody struggles of his country for freedom and existence, till "a Scottish prejudice," he says, "was poured into my veins, which will boil there till the flood-gates of life are shut in eternal rest."

In this mood of mind Burns was unconsciously approaching the land of poesie. In addition to the histories of the Wallace and the Bruce, he found, on the shelves of his neighbours, not only whole bodies of divinity, and sermons without limit, but the works of some of the best English, as well as Scottish poets, together with songs and ballads innumerable. On these he loved to pore whenever a moment of leisure came; nor was verse his sole favourite; he desired to drink knowledge at any fountain, and Guthrie's Grammar, Dickson on Agriculture, Addison's Spectator, Locke on the Human Understanding, and Taylor's Scripture Doctrine of Original Sin, were as welcome to his heart as Shakspeare, Milton, Pope, Thomson, and Young. There is a mystery in the workings of genius: with these poets in his head and hand, we see not that he has advanced one step in the way in which he was soon to walk, "Highland Mary" and "Tam O' Shanter" sprang from other inspirations.

Burns lifts up the veil himself, from the studies which made him a poet. "In my boyish days," he says to Moore, "I owed much to an old woman (Jenny Wilson) who resided in the family, remarkable for her credulity and superstition. She had, I suppose, the largest collection in the country of tales and songs, concerning devils, ghosts, fairies, brownies, witches, warlocks, spunkies, kelpies, elf-candles, dead-lights, wraiths, apparitions, cantraips, giants, enchanted towers, dragons, and other trumpery. This cultivated the latent seeds of poesie; but had so strong an effect upon my imagination that to this hour, in my nocturnal rambles, I sometimes keep a look-out on suspicious places." Here we have the young poet taking lessons in the classic lore of his native land: in the school of Janet Wilson he profited largely; her tales gave a hue, all their own, to many noble effusions. But her teaching was at the hearth-stone: when he was in the fields, either driving a cart or walking to labour, he had ever in his hand a collection of songs, such as any stall in the land could supply him with; and over these he pored, ballad by ballad, and verse by verse, noting the true, tender, and the natural sublime from affectation and fustian. "To this," he said, "I am convinced that I owe much of my critic craft, such as it is." His mother, too, unconsciously led him in the ways of the muse: she loved to recite or sing to him a strange, but clever ballad, called "the Life and Age of Man:" this strain of piety and imagination was in his mind when he wrote "Man was made to Mourn."

He found other teachers — of a tenderer nature and softer influence. "You know," he says to Moore, "our country custom of coupling a man and woman together as partners in the labours of harvest. In my fifteenth autumn my partner was a bewitching creature, a year younger than myself: she was in truth a bonnie, sweet, sonsie lass, and unwittingly to herself, initiated me in that delicious passion, which, in spite of acid disappointment, gin-horse prudence, and bookworm philosophy, I hold to be the first of human joys. How she caught the contagion I cannot tell; I never expressly said I loved her: indeed I did not know myself why I liked so much to loiter behind with her, when returning in the evenings from our labours; why the tones of her voice made my heart strings thrill like an Æolian harp, and particularly why my pulse beat such a furious ratan, when I looked and fingered over her little hand, to pick out the cruel nettle-stings and thistles. Among other love-inspiring qualities, she sang sweetly, and it was her favourite reel to which I attempted to give an embodied vehicle in rhyme; thus with me began love and verse." This intercourse with the fair part of the creation, was to his slumbering emotions, a voice from heaven to call them into life and poetry.

From the school of traditionary lore and love, Burns now went to a rougher academy. Lochlea, though not producing fine crops of corn, was considered excellent for flax; and while the cultivation of this commodity was committed to his father and his brother Gilbert, he was sent to Irvine at Midsummer, 1781, to learn the trade of a flax-dresser, under one Peacock, kinsman to his mother. Some time before, he had spent a portion of a summer at a school in Kirkoswald, learning mensuration and land-surveying, where he had mingled in scenes of sociality with smugglers, and enjoyed the pleasure of a silent walk, under the moon, with the young and the beautiful. At Irvine he laboured by day to acquire a knowledge of his business, and at night he associated with the gay and the thoughtless, with whom he learnt to empty his glass, and indulge in free discourse on topics forbidden at Lochlea. He had one small room for a lodging, for which he gave a shilling a week: meat he seldom tasted, and his food consisted chiefly of oatmeal and potatoes sent from his father's house. In a letter to his father, written with great purity and simplicity of style, he thus gives a picture of himself, mental and bodily: "Honoured Sir, I have purposely delayed writing, in the hope that I should have the pleasure of seeing you on new years' day, but work comes so hard upon us that I do not choose to be absent on that account. My health is nearly the same as when you were here, only my sleep is a little sounder, and on the whole, I am rather better than otherwise, though I mend by very slow degrees: the weakness of my nerves had so debilitated my mind that I dare neither review past wants nor look forward into futurity, for the least anxiety or perturbation in my breast produces most unhappy effects on my whole frame. Sometimes indeed, when for an hour or two my spirits are a little lightened, I *glimmer* a little into futurity; but my principal and indeed my only pleasurable employment is looking backwards and forwards in a moral and religious way. I am quite transported at the thought that ere long, perhaps very soon, I shall bid an eternal adieu to all the pains and uneasinesses, and disquietudes of this weary life. As for the world, I despair of ever making a figure in it: I am not formed for the bustle of the busy, nor the flutter of the gay. I foresee that poverty and obscurity probably await me, and I am in some measure prepared and daily preparing to meet them. I have but just time and paper to return you my grateful thanks for the lessons of virtue and piety you have given me, which were but too much neglected at the time of giving them, but which, I hope, have been remembered ere it is yet too late." This remarkable letter was written in the twenty-second year of his age; it alludes to the illness which seems to have been the companion of his youth, a nervous headache, brought on by constant toil and anxiety; and it speaks of the melancholy which is the common attendant of genius, and its sensibilities, aggravated by despair of distinction. The catastrophe which happened ere this letter was well in his father's hand, accords ill with quotations from the Bible, and hopes fixed in heaven:—"As we gave," he says, "a welcome carousal to the new year, the shop took fire, and burnt to ashes, and I was left, like a true poet, not worth a sixpence."

This disaster was followed by one more grievous: his father was well in years when he was married, and age and a constitution injured by toil and disappointment, began to press him down, ere his sons had grown up to man's estate. On all sides the clouds began to darken: the farm was unprosperous: the speculations in flax failed; and the landlord of Lochlea, raising a question upon the meaning of the lease, concerning rotation of crop, pushed the matter to a lawsuit, alike ruinous to a poor man either in its success or its failure. "After three years tossing and whirling," says Burns, "in the vortex of litigation, my father was just saved from the horrors of a jail by a consumption, which, after two years' promises, kindly slept in and carried him away to where the 'wicked cease from troubling and the weary are at rest.' His all went among the hell-hounds that prowl in the kennel of justice. The finishing evil which brought up the rear of this infernal file, was my constitutional melancholy being increased to such a degree, that for three months I was in a state of mind scarcely to be envied by the hopeless wretches who have got their mittimus, 'Depart from me, ye cursed.'"

Robert Burns was now the head of his father's house. He gathered together the little that law and misfortune had spared, and took the farm of Mossgiel, near Mauchline, containing one hundred and eighteen acres, at a rent of ninety pounds a year: his mother and sisters took the domestic superintendence of home, barn, and byre; and he associated his brother Gilbert in the labours of the land. It was made a joint affair: the poet was young, willing, and vigorous, and excelled in ploughing, sowing, reaping, mowing, and thrashing. His wages were fixed at seven pounds per annum, and such for a time was his care and frugality, that he never exceeded this small allowance. He purchased books on farming, held conversations with the old and the knowing; and said unto himself, "I shall be prudent and wise, and my shadow shall increase in the land." But it was not decreed that these resolutions were to endure, and that he was to become a mighty agriculturist in the west. Farmer Attention, as the proverb says, is a good farmer, all the world over, and Burns was such by fits and by starts. But he who writes an ode on the sheep he is about to shear, a poem on the flower that he covers with the furrow, who sees visions on his way to market, who makes rhymes on the horse he is about to yoke, and a song on the girl who shows the whitest hands among his reapers, has small chance of leading a market, or of being laird of the fields he rents. The dreams of Burns were of the muses, and not of rising markets, of golden locks rather than of yellow corn: he had other faults. It is not known that William Burns was aware before his death that his eldest son had sinned in rhyme; but we have Gilbert's assurance, that his father went to the grave in ignorance of his son's errors of a less venial kind — unwitting that he was soon to give a two-fold proof of both in "Rob the Rhymer's Address to his Bastard Child"— a poem less decorous than witty.

The dress and condition of Burns when he became a poet were not at all poetical, in the minstrel meaning of the word. His clothes, coarse and homely, were made from home-grown wool, shorn off his own sheeps' backs, carded and spun at his own fireside, woven by the village weaver, and, when not of natural hodden-gray, dyed a half-blue in the village vat. They were shaped and sewed by the district tailor, who usually wrought at the rate of a groat a day and his food; and as the wool was coarse, so also was the workmanship. The linen which he wore was home-grown, home-hackled, home-spun, home-woven, and home-bleached, and, unless designed for Sunday use, was of coarse, strong harn, to suit the tear and wear of barn and field. His shoes came from rustic tanpits, for most farmers then prepared their own leather; were armed, sole and heel, with heavy, broad-headed nails, to endure the clod and the road: as hats were then little in use, save among small lairds or country gentry, westland heads were commonly covered with a coarse, broad, blue bonnet, with a stopple on its flat crown, made in thousands at Kilmarnock, and known in all lands by the name of scone bonnets. His plaid was a handsome red and white check — for pride in poets, he said, was no sin — prepared of fine wool with more than common care by the hands of his mother and sisters, and woven with more skill than the village weaver was usually required to exert. His dwelling was in keeping with his dress, a low, thatched house, with a kitchen, a bedroom and closet, with floors of kneaded clay, and ceilings of moorland turf: a few books on a shelf, thumbed by many a thumb; a few hams drying above head in the smoke, which was in no haste to get out at the roof — a wooden settle, some oak chairs, chaff beds well covered with blankets, with a fire of peat and wood burning at a distance from the gable wall, on the middle of the floor. His food was as homely as his habitation, and consisted chiefly of oatmeal-porridge, barley-broth, and potatoes, and milk. How the muse happened to visit him in this clay biggin, take a fancy to a clouterly peasant, and teach him strains of consummate beauty and elegance, must ever be a matter of wonder to all those, and they are not few, who hold that noble sentiments and heroic deeds are the exclusive portion of the gently nursed and the far descended.

Of the earlier verses of Burns few are preserved: when composed, he put them on paper, but the kept them to himself: though a poet at sixteen, he seems not to have made even his brother his confidante till he became a man, and his judgment had ripened. He, however, made a little clasped paper book his treasurer, and under the head of "Observations, Hints, Songs, and Scraps of Poetry," we find many a wayward and impassioned verse, songs rising little above the humblest country strain, or bursting into an elegance and a beauty worthy of the highest of minstrels. The first words noted down are the stanzas which he composed on his fair companion of the harvest-field, out of whose hands he loved to remove the nettle-stings and the thistles: the prettier song, beginning "Now westlin win's and slaughtering guns," written on the lass of Kirkoswald, with whom, instead of learning mensuration, he chose to wander under the light of the moon: a strain better still, inspired by the charms of a neighbouring maiden, of the name of Annie Ronald; another, of equal merit, arising out of his nocturnal adventures among the lasses of the west; and, finally, that crowning glory of all his lyric compositions, "Green grow the rashes." This little clasped book, however, seems not to have been made his confidante till his twenty-third or twenty-fourth year: he probably admitted to its pages only the strains which he loved most, or such as had taken a place in his memory: at whatever age it was commenced, he had then begun to estimate his own character, and intimate his fortunes, for he calls himself in its pages "a man who had little art in making money, and still less in keeping it."

We have not been told how welcome the incense of his songs rendered him to the rustic maidens of Kyle: women are not apt to be won by the charms of verse; they have little sympathy with dreamers on Parnassus, and allow themselves to be influenced by something more substantial than the roses and lilies of the muse. Burns had other claims to their regard then those arising from poetic skill: he was tall, young, good-looking, with dark, bright eyes, and words and wit at will: he had a sarcastic sally for all lads who presumed to cross his path, and a soft, persuasive word for all lasses on whom he fixed his fancy: nor was this all — he was adventurous and bold in love trysts and love excursions: long, rough roads, stormy nights, flooded rivers, and lonesome places, were no letts to him; and when the dangers or labours of the way were braved, he was alike skilful in eluding vigilant aunts, wakerife mothers, and envious or suspicions sisters: for rivals he had a blow as ready us he had a word, and was familiar with snug stack-yards, broomy glens, and nooks of hawthorn and honeysuckle, where maidens love to be wooed. This rendered him dearer to woman's heart than all the lyric effusions of his fancy; and when we add to such allurements, a warm, flowing, and persuasive eloquence, we need not wonder that woman listened and was won; that one of the most charming damsels of the West said, an hour with him in the dark was worth a lifetime of light with any other body; or that the accomplished and beautiful Duchess of Gordon declared, in a latter day, that no man ever carried her so completely off her feet as Robert Burns.

It is one of the delusions of the poet's critics and biographers, that the sources of his inspiration are to be found in the great classic poets of the land, with some of whom he had from his youth been familiar: there is little or no trace of them in any of his compositions. He read and wondered — he warmed his fancy at their flame, he corrected his own natural taste by theirs, but he neither copied nor imitated, and there are but two or three allusions to Young and Shakspeare in all the range of his verse. He could not but feel that he was the scholar of a different school, and that his thirst was to be slaked at other fountains. The language in which those great bards embodied their thoughts was unapproachable to an Ayrshire peasant; it was to him as an almost foreign tongue: he had to think and feel in the not ungraceful or inharmonious language of his own vale, and then, in a manner, translate it into that of Pope or of Thomson, with the additional difficulty of finding English words to express the exact meaning of those of Scotland, which had chiefly been retained because equivalents could not be found in the more elegant and grammatical tongue. Such strains as those of the polished Pope or the sublimer Milton were beyond his power, less from deficiency of genius than from lack of language: he could, indeed, write English with ease and fluency; but when he desired to be tender or impassioned, to persuade or subdue, he had recourse to the Scottish, and he found it sufficient.

The goddesses or the Dalilahs of the young poet's song were, like the language in which he celebrated them, the produce of the district; not dames high and exalted, but lasses of the barn and of the byre, who had never been in higher company than that of shepherds or ploughmen, or danced in a politer assembly than that of their fellow-peasants, on a barn-floor, to the sound of the district fiddle. Nor even of these did he choose the loveliest to lay out the wealth of his verse upon: he has been accused, by his brother among others, of lavishing the colours of his fancy on very ordinary faces. "He had always," says Gilbert, "a jealousy of people who were richer than himself; his love, therefore, seldom settled on persons of this description. When he selected any one, out of the sovereignty of his good pleasure, to whom he should pay his particular attention, she was instantly invested with a sufficient stock of charms out of the plentiful stores of his own imagination: and there was often a great dissimilitude between his fair captivator, as she appeared to others and as she seemed when invested with the attributes he gave her." "My heart," he himself, speaking of those days, observes, "was completely tinder, and was eternally lighted up by some goddess or other." Yet, it must be acknowledged that sufficient room exists for believing that Burns and his brethren of the West had very different notions of the captivating and the beautiful; while they were moved by rosy checks and looks of rustic health, he was moved, like a sculptor, by beauty of form or by harmony of motion, and by expression, which lightened up ordinary features and rendered them captivating. Such, I have been told, were several of the lasses of the West, to whom, if he did not surrender his heart, he rendered homage: and both elegance of form and beauty of face were visible to all in those of whom he afterwards sang — the Hamiltons and the Burnets of Edinburgh, and the Millers and M'Murdos of the Nith.

The mind of Burns took now a wider range: he had sung of the maidens of Kyle in strains not likely soon to die, and though not weary of the softnesses of love, he desired to try his genius on matters of a sterner kind — what those subjects were he tells us; they were homely and at hand, of a native nature and of Scottish growth: places celebrated in Roman story, vales made famous in Grecian song — hills of vines and groves of myrtle had few charms for him. "I am hurt," thus he writes in August, 1785, "to see other towns, rivers, woods, and haughs of Scotland immortalized in song, while my dear native county, the ancient Baillieries of Carrick, Kyle, and Cunningham, famous in both ancient and modern times for a gallant and warlike race of inhabitants — a county where civil and religious liberty have ever found their first support and their asylum — a county, the birth-place of many famous philosophers, soldiers, and statesmen, and the scene of many great events recorded in history, particularly the actions of the glorious Wallace — yet we have never had one Scotch poet of any eminence to make the fertile banks of Irvine, the romantic woodlands and sequestered scenes of Ayr. and the mountainous source and winding sweep of the Doon, emulate Tay, Forth, Ettrick, and Tweed. This is a complaint I would gladly remedy, but, alas! I am far unequal to the task, both in genius and education." To fill up with glowing verse the outline which this sketch indicates, was to raise the long-laid spirit of national song — to waken a strain to which the whole land would yield response — a miracle unattempted — certainly unperformed — since the days of the Gentle Shepherd. It is true that the tongue of the muse had at no time been wholly silent; that now and then a burst of sublime woe, like the song of "Mary, weep no more for me," and of lasting merriment and humour, like that of "Tibbie Fowler," proved that the fire of natural poesie smouldered, if it did not blaze; while the social strains of the unfortunate Fergusson revived in the city, if not in the field, the memory of him who sang the "Monk and the Miller's wife." But notwithstanding these and other productions of equal merit, Scottish poesie, it must be owned, had lost much of its original ecstasy and fervour, and that the boldest efforts of the muse no more equalled the songs of Dunbar, of Douglas, of Lyndsay, and of James the Fifth, than the sound of an artificial cascade resembles the undying thunders of Corra.

To accomplish this required an acquaintance with man beyond what the forge, the change-house, and the market-place of the village supplied; a look further than the barn-yard and the furrowed field, and a livelier knowledge and deeper feeling of history than, probably, Burns ever possessed. To all ready and accessible sources of knowledge he appears to have had recourse; he sought matter for his muse in the meetings, religious as well as social, of the district — consorted with staid matrons, grave plodding farmers — with those who preached as well as those who listened — with sharp-tongued attorneys, who laid down the law over a Mauchline gill — with country squires, whose wisdom was great in the game-laws, and in contested elections — and with roving smugglers, who at that time hung, as a cloud, on all the western coast of Scotland. In the company of farmers and fellow-peasants, he witnessed scenes which he loved to embody in verse, saw pictures of peace and joy, now woven into the web of his song, and had a poetic impulse given to him both by cottage devotion and cottage merriment. If he was familiar with love and all its outgoings and incomings — had met his lass in the midnight shade, or walked with her under the moon, or braved a stormy night and a haunted road for her sake — he was as well acquainted with the joys which belong to social intercourse, when instruments of music speak to the feet, when the reek of punchbowls gives a tongue to the staid and demure, and bridal festivity, and harvest-homes, bid a whole valley lift up its voice and be glad. It is more difficult to decide what poetic use he could make of his intercourse with that loose and lawless class of men, who, from love of gain, broke the laws and braved the police of their country: that he found among smugglers, as he says, "men of noble virtues, magnanimity, generosity, disinterested friendship, and modesty," is easier to believe than that he escaped the contamination of their sensual manners and prodigality. The people of Kyle regarded this conduct with suspicion: they were not to be expected to know that when Burns ranted and housed with smugglers, conversed with tinkers huddled in a kiln, or listened to the riotous mirth of a batch of "randie gangrel bodies" as they "toomed their powks and pawned their duds," for liquor in Poosie Nansie's, he was taking sketches for the future entertainment and instruction of the world; they could not foresee that from all this moral strength and poetic beauty would arise.

While meditating something better than a ballad to his mistress's eyebrow, he did not neglect to lay out the little skill he had in cultivating the grounds of Mossgiel. The prosperity in which he found himself in the first and second seasons, induced him to hope that good fortune had not yet forsaken him: a genial summer and a good market seldom come together to the farmer, but at first they came to Burns; and to show that he was worthy of them, he bought books on agriculture, calculated rotation of crops, attended sales, held the plough with diligence, used the scythe, the reap-hook, and the flail, with skill, and the malicious even began to say that there was something more in him than wild sallies of wit and foolish rhymes. But the farm lay high, the bottom was wet, and in a third season, indifferent seed and a wet harvest robbed him at once of half his crop: he seems to have regarded this as an intimation from above, that nothing which he undertook would prosper: and consoled himself with joyous friends and with the society of the muse. The judgment cannot be praised which selected a farm with a wet cold bottom, and sowed it with unsound seed; but that man who despairs because a wet season robs him of the fruits of the field, is unfit for the warfare of life, where fortitude is as much required as by a general on a field of battle, when the tide of success threatens to flow against him. The poet seems to have believed, very early in life, that he was none of the elect of Mammon; that he was too much of a genius ever to acquire wealth by steady labour, or by, as he loved to call it, gin-horse prudence, or grubbing industry.

And yet there were hours and days in which Burns, even when the rain fell on his unhoused sheaves, did not wholly despair of himself: he laboured, nay sometimes he slaved on his farm; and at intervals of toil, sought to embellish his mind with such knowledge as might be useful, should chance, the goddess who ruled his lot, drop him upon some of the higher places of the land. He had, while he lived at Tarbolton, united with some half-dozen young men, all sons of farmers in that neighbourhood, in forming a club, of which the object was to charm away a few evening hours in the week with agreeable chit-chat, and the discussion of topics of economy or love. Of this little society the poet was president, and the first question they were called on to settle was this, "Suppose a young man bred a farmer, but without any fortune, has it in his power to marry either of two women; the one a girl of large fortune, but neither handsome in person, nor agreeable in conversation, but who can manage the household affairs of a farm well enough; the other of them, a girl every way agreeable in person, conversation, and behaviour, but without any fortune, which of them shall he choose?" This question was started by the poet, and once every week the club were called to the consideration of matters connected with rural life and industry: their expenses were limited to threepence a week; and till the departure of Burns to the distant Mossgiel, the club continued to live and thrive; on his removal it lost the spirit which gave it birth, and was heard of no more; but its aims and its usefulness were revived in Mauchline, where the poet was induced to establish a society which only differed from the other in spending the moderate fines arising from non-attendance, on books, instead of liquor. Here, too, Burns was the president, and the members were chiefly the sons of husbandmen, whom he found, he said, more natural in their manners, and more agreeable than the self-sufficient mechanics of villages and towns, who were ready to dispute on all topics, and inclined to be convinced on none. This club had the pleasure of subscribing for the first edition of the works of its great associate. It has been questioned by his first biographer, whether the refinement of mind, which follows the reading of books of eloquence and delicacy — the mental improvement resulting from such calm discussions as the Tarbolton and Mauchline clubs indulged in, was not injurious to men engaged in the barn and at the plough. A well-ordered mind will be strengthened, as well as embellished, by elegant knowledge, while over those naturally barren and ungenial all that is refined or noble will pass as a sunny shower scuds over lumps of granite, bringing neither warmth nor life.

In the account which the poet gives to Moore of his early poems, he says little about his exquisite lyrics, and less about "The Death and dying Words of Poor Mailie," or her "Elegy," the first of his poems where the inspiration of the muse is visible; but he speaks with exultation of the fame which those indecorous sallies, "Holy Willie's Prayer" and "The Holy Tulzie" brought from some of the clergy, and the people of Ayrshire. The west of Scotland is ever in the van, when mutters either political or religious are agitated. Calvinism was shaken, at this time, with a controversy among its professors, of which it is enough to say, that while one party rigidly adhered to the word and letter of the Confession of Faith, and preached up the palmy and wholesome days of the Covenant, the other sought to soften the harsher rules and observances of the kirk, and to bring moderation and charity into its discipline as well as its councils. Both believed themselves right, both were loud and hot, and personal — bitter with a bitterness only known in religious controversy. The poet sided with the professors of the New Light, as the more tolerant were called, and handled the professors of the Old Light, as the other party were named, with the most unsparing severity. For this he had sufficient cause:— he had experienced the mercilessness of kirk-discipline, when his frailties caused him to visit the stool of repentance; and moreover his friend Gavin Hamilton, a writer in Mauchline, had been sharply censured by the same authorities, for daring to gallop on Sundays. Moodie, of Riccarton, and Russel, of Kilmarnock, were the first who tasted of the poet's wrath. They, though professors of the Old Light, had quarrelled, and, it is added, fought: "The Holy Tulzie," which recorded, gave at the same time wings to the scandal; while for "Holy Willie," an elder of Mauchline, and an austere and hollow pretender to righteousness, he reserved the fiercest of all his lampoons. In "Holy Willie's Prayer," he lays a burning hand on the terrible doctrine of predestination: this is a satire, daring, personal, and profane. Willie claims praise in the singular, acknowledges folly in the plural, and makes heaven accountable for his sins! in a similar strain of undevout satire, he congratulates Goudie, of Kilmarnock, on his Essays on Revealed Religion. These poems, particularly the two latter, are the sharpest lampoons in the language.

While drudging in the cause of the New Light controversialists, Burns was not unconsciously strengthening his hands for worthier toils: the applause which selfish divines bestowed on his witty, but graceless effusions, could not be enough for one who knew how fleeting the fame was which came from the heat of party disputes; nor was he insensible that songs of a beauty unknown for a century to national poesy, had been unregarded in the hue and cry which arose on account of "Holy Willie's Prayer" and "The Holy Tulzie." He hesitated to drink longer out of the agitated puddle of Calvinistic controversy, he resolved to slake his thirst at the pure well-springs of patriot feeling and domestic love; and accordingly, in the last and best of his controversial compositions, he rose out of the lower regions of lampoon into the upper air of true poetry. "The Holy Fair," though stained in one or two verses with personalities, exhibits a scene glowing with character and incident and life: the aim of the poem is not so much to satirize one or two Old Light divines, as to expose and rebuke those almost indecent festivities, which in too many of the western parishes accompanied the administration of the sacrament. In the earlier days of the church, when men were staid and sincere, it was, no doubt, an impressive sight to see rank succeeding rank, of the old and the young, all calm and all devout, seated before the tent of the preacher, in the sunny hours of June, listening to his eloquence, or partaking of the mystic bread and wine; but in these our latter days, when discipline is relaxed, along with the sedate and the pious come swarms of the idle and the profligate, whom no eloquence can edify and no solemn rite affect. On these, and such as these, the poet has poured his satire; and since this desirable reprehension the Holy Fairs, east as well as west, have become more decorous, if not more devout.

His controversial sallies were accompanied, or followed, by a series of poems which showed that national character and manners, as Lockhart has truly and happily said, were once more in the hands of a national poet. These compositions are both numerous and various: they record the poet's own experience and emotions; they exhibit the highest moral feeling, the purest patriotic sentiments, and a deep sympathy with the fortunes, both here and hereafter of his fellow-men; they delineate domestic manners, man's stern as well as social hours, and mingle the serious with the joyous, the sarcastic with the solemn, the mournful with the pathetic, the amiable with the gay, and all with an ease and unaffected force and freedom known only to the genius of Shakspeare. In "The Twa Dogs" he seeks to reconcile the labourer to his lot, and intimates, by examples drawn from the hall as well as the cottage, that happiness resides in the humblest abodes, and is even partial to the clouted shoe. In "Scotch Drink" he excites man to love his country, by precepts both heroic and social; and proves that while wine and brandy are the tipple of slaves, whiskey and ale are the drink of the free: sentiments of a similar kind distinguish his "Earnest Cry and Prayer to the Scotch Representatives in the House of Commons," each of whom he exhorts by name to defend the remaining liberties and immunities of his country. A higher tone distinguishes the "Address to the Deil:" he records all the names, and some of them are strange ones; and all the acts, and some of them are as whimsical as they are terrible, of this far kenned and noted personage; to these he adds some of the fiend's doings as they stand in Scripture, together with his own experiences; and concludes by a hope, as unexpected as merciful and relenting, that Satan may not be exposed to an eternity of torments. "The Dream" is a humorous sally, and may be almost regarded as prophetic. The poet feigns himself present, in slumber, at the Royal birth-day; and supposes that he addresses his majesty, on his household matters as well as the affairs of the nation. Some of the princes, it has been satirically hinted, behaved afterwards in such a way as if they wished that the scripture of the Burns should be fulfilled: in this strain, he has imitated the license and equalled the wit of some of the elder Scottish Poets.

"The Vision" is wholly serious; it exhibits the poet in one of those fits of despondency which the dull, who have no misgivings, never know: he dwells with sarcastic bitterness on the opportunities which, for the sake of song, he has neglected of becoming wealthy, and is drawing a sad parallel between rags and riches, when the muse steps in and cheer his despondency, by assuring him of undying fame. "Halloween" is a strain of a more homely kind, recording the superstitious beliefs, and no less superstitious doings of Old Scotland, on that night, when witches and elves and evil spirits are let loose among the children of men: it reaches far back into manners and customs, and is a picture, curious and valuable. The tastes and feelings of husbandmen inspired "The old Farmer's Address to his old mare Maggie," which exhibits some pleasing recollections of his days of courtship and hours of sociality. The calm, tranquil picture of household happiness and devotion in "the Cotter's Saturday Night," has induced Hogg, among others, to believe that it has less than usual of the spirit of the poet, but it has all the spirit that was required; the toil of the week has ceased, the labourer has returned to his well-ordered home — his "cozie ingle and his clean hearth-stane,"— and with his wife and children beside him, turns his thoughts to the praise of that God to whom he owes all: this he performs with a reverence and an awe, at once natural, national, and poetic. "The Mouse" is a brief and happy and very moving poem: happy, for it delineates, with wonderful truth and life, the agitation of the mouse when the coulter broke into its abode; and moving, for the poet takes the lesson of ruin to himself, and feels the present and dreads the future. "The Mountain Daisy," once, more properly, called by Burns "The Gowan," resembles "The Mouse" in incident and in moral, and is equally happy, in language and conception. "The Lament" is a dark, and all but tragic page, from the poet's own life. "Man was made to Mourn'" takes the part of the humble and the homeless, against the coldness and selfishness of the wealthy and the powerful, a favourite topic of meditation with Burns. He refrained, for awhile, from making "Death and Doctor Hernbook" public; a poem which deviates from the offensiveness of personal satire, into a strain of humour, at once airy and original.

His epistles in verse may be reckoned amongst his happiest productions: they are written in all moods of mind, and are, by turns, lively and sad; careless and serious; — now giving advice, then taking it; laughing at learning, and lamenting its want; scoffing at propriety and wealth, yet admitting, that without the one he cannot be wise, nor wanting the other, independent. The Epistle to David Sillar is the first of these compositions: the poet has no news to tell, and no serious question to ask: he has only to communicate his own emotions of joy, or of sorrow, and these he relates and discusses with singular elegance as well as ease, twining, at the same time, into the fabric of his composition, agreeable allusions to the taste and affections of his correspondent. He seems to have rated the intellect of Sillar as the highest among his rustic friends: he pays him more deference, and addresses him in a higher vein than he observes to others. The Epistles to Lapraik, to Smith, and to Rankine, are in a more familiar, or social mood, and lift the veil from the darkness of the poet's condition, and exhibit a mind of first-rate power, groping, and that surely, its way to distinction, in spite of humility of birth, obscurity of condition, and the coldness of the wealthy or the titled. The epistles of other poets owe some of their fame to the rank or the reputation of those to whom they are addressed; those of Burns are written, one and all, to nameless and undistinguished men. Sillar was a country schoolmaster, Lapraik a moorland laird, Smith a small shop-keeper, and Rankine a farmer, who loved a gill and a joke. Yet these men were the chief friends, the only literary associates of the poet, during those early years, in which, with some exceptions, his finest works were written.

Burns, while he was writing the poems, the chief of which we have named, was a labouring husbandman on the little farm of Mossgiel, a pursuit which affords but few leisure hours for either reading or pondering; but to him the stubble-field was musing-ground, and the walk behind the plough, a twilight saunter on Parnassus. As, with a careful hand and a steady eye, he guided his horses, and saw an evenly furrow turned up by the share, his thoughts were on other themes; he was straying in haunted glens, when spirits have power — looking in fancy on the lasses "skelping barefoot," in silks and in scarlets, to a field-preaching — walking in imagination with the rosy widow, who on Halloween ventured to dip her left sleeve in the burn, where three lairds' lands met — making the "bottle clunk," with joyous smugglers, on a lucky run of gin or brandy — or if his thoughts at all approached his acts — he was moralizing on the daisy oppressed by the furrow which his own ploughshare had turned. That his thoughts were thus wandering we have his own testimony, with that of his brother Gilbert; and were both wanting, the certainty that he composed the greater part of his immortal poems in two years, from the summer of 1784 to the summer of 1786, would be evidence sufficient. The muse must have been strong within him, when, in spite of the rains and sleets of the "ever-dropping west"— when in defiance of the hot and sweaty brows occasioned by reaping and thrashing — declining markets, and showery harvests — the clamour of his laird for his rent, and the tradesman for his account, he persevered in song, and sought solace in verse, when all other solace was denied him.

The circumstances under which his principal poems were composed, have been related: the "Lament of Mailie" found its origin in the catastrophe of a pet ewe; the "Epistle to Sillar" was confided by the poet to his brother while they were engaged in weeding the kale-yard; the "Address to the Deil" was suggested by the many strange portraits which belief or fear had drawn of Satan, and was repeated by the one brother to the other, on the way with their carts to the kiln, for lime; the "Cotter's Saturday Night" originated in the reverence with which the worship of God was conducted in the family of the poet's father, and in the solemn tone with which he desired his children to compose themselves for praise and prayer; "the Mouse," and its moral companion "the Daisy," were the offspring of the incidents which they relate; and "Death and Doctor Hornbook" was conceived at a freemason-meeting, where the hero of the piece had shown too much of the pedant, and composed on his way home, after midnight, by the poet, while his head was somewhat dizzy with drink. One of the most remarkable of his compositions, the "Jolly Beggars," a drama, to which nothing in the language of either the North or South can be compared, and which was unknown till after the death of the author, was suggested by a scene which he saw in a low ale-house, into which, on a Saturday night, most of the sturdy beggars of the district had met to sell their meal, pledge their superfluous rags, and drink their gains. It may be added, that he loved to walk in solitary spots; that his chief musing-ground was the banks of the Ayr; the season most congenial to his fancy that of winter, when the winds were heard in the leafless woods, and the voice of the swollen streams came from vale and hill; and that he seldom composed a whole poem at once, but satisfied with a few fervent verses, laid the subject aside, till the muse summoned him to another exertion of fancy. In a little back closet, still existing in the farm-house of Mossgiel, he committed most of his poems to paper.

But while the poet rose, the farmer sank. It was not the cold clayey bottom of his ground, nor the purchase of unsound seed-corn, not the fluctuation in the markets alone, which injured him; neither was it the taste for freemason socialities, nor a desire to join the mirth of comrades, either of the sea or the shore: neither could it be wholly imputed to his passionate following of the softer sex — indulgence in the "illicit rove," or giving way to his eloquence at the feet of one whom he loved and honoured; other farmers indulged in the one, or suffered from the other, yet were prosperous. His want of success arose from other causes; his heart was not with his task, save by fits and starts: he felt he was designed for higher purposes than ploughing, and harrowing, and sowing, and reaping: when the sun called on him, after a shower, to come to the plough, or when the ripe corn invited the sickle, or the ready market called for the measured grain, the poet was under other spells, and was slow to avail himself of those golden moments which come but once in the season. To this may be added, a too superficial knowledge of the art of farming, and a want of intimacy with the nature of the soil he was called to cultivate. He could speak fluently of leas, and faughs, and fallows, of change of seed and rotation of crops, but practical knowledge and application were required, and in these Burns was deficient. The moderate gain which those dark days of agriculture brought to the economical farmer, was not obtained: the close, the all but niggardly care by which he could win and keep his crown-piece — gold was seldom in the farmer's hand — was either above or below the mind of the poet, and Mossgiel, which, in the hands of an assiduous farmer, might have made a reasonable return for labour, was unproductive, under one who had little skill, less economy, and no taste for the task.

Other reasons for his failure have been assigned. It is to the credit of the moral sentiments of the husbandmen of Scotland, that when one of their class forgets what virtue requires, and dishonours, without reparation, even the humblest of the maidens, he is not allowed to go unpunished. No proceedings take place, perhaps one hard word is not spoken; but he is regarded with loathing by the old and the devout; he is looked on by all with cold and reproachful eyes — sorrow is foretold as his lot, sure disaster as his fortune; and is these chance to arrive, the only sympathy expressed is, "What better could he expect?" Something of this sort befel Burns: he had already satisfied the kirk in the matter of "Sonsie, smirking, dear-bought Bess," his daughter, by one of his mother's maids; and now, to use his own words, he was brought within point-blank of the heaviest metal of the kirk by a similar folly. The fair transgressor, both for her fathers and her own youth, had a large share of public sympathy. Jean Armour, for it is of her I speak, was in her eighteenth year; with dark eyes, a handsome foot, and a melodious tongue, she made her way to the poet's heart — and, as their stations in life were equal, it seemed that they had only to be satisfied themselves to render their union easy. But her father, in addition to being a very devout man, was a zealot of the Old Light; and Jean, dreading his resentment, was willing, while she loved its unforgiven satirist, to love him in secret, in the hope that the time would come when she might safely avow it: she admitted the poet, therefore, to her company in lonesome places, and walks beneath the moon, where they both forgot themselves, and were at last obliged to own a private marriage as a protection from kirk censure. The professors of the Old Light rejoiced, since it brought a scoffing rhymer within reach of their hand; but her father felt a twofold sorrow, because of the shame of a favourite daughter, and for having committed the folly with one both loose in conduct and profane of speech. He had cause to be angry, but his anger, through his zeal, became tyrannous: in the exercise of what he called a father's power, he compelled his child to renounce the poet as her husband and burn the marriage-lines; for he regarded her marriage, without the kirk's permission, with a man so utterly cast away, as a worse crime than her folly. So blind is anger! She could renounce neither her husband nor his offspring in a lawful way, and in spite of the destruction of the marriage lines, and renouncing the name of wife, she was as much Mrs. Burns as marriage could make her. No one concerned seemed to think so. Burns, who loved her tenderly, went all but mad when she renounced him: he gave up his share of Mossgiel to his brother, and roamed, moody and idle, about the land, with no better aim in life than a situation in one of our western sugar-isles, and a vague hope of distinction as a poet.

How the distinction which he desired as a poet was to be obtained, was, to a poor bard in a provincial place, a sore puzzle: there were no enterprising booksellers in the western land, and it was not to be expected that the printers of either Kilmarnock or Paisley had money to expend on a speculation in rhyme: it is much to the honour of his native county that the publication which he wished for was at last made easy. The best of his poems, in his own handwriting, had found their way into the hands of the Ballantynes, Hamiltons, Parkers, and Mackenzies, and were much admired. Mrs. Stewart, of Stair and Afton, a lady of distinction and taste, had made, accidentally, the acquaintance both of Burns and some of his songs, and was ready to befriend him; and so favourable was the impression on all hands, that a subscription, sufficient to defray the outlay of paper and print, was soon filled up — one hundred copies being subscribed for by the Parkers alone. He soon arranged materials for a volume, and put them into the hands of a printer in Kilmarnock, the Wee Johnnie of one of his biting epigrams. Johnnie was startled at the unceremonious freedom of most of the pieces, and asked the poet to compose one of modest language and moral aim, to stand at the beginning, and excuse some of those free ones which followed: Burns, whose "Twa Dogs" was then incomplete, finished the poem at a sitting, and put it in the van, much to his printer's satisfaction. If the "Jolly Beggars" was omitted for any other cause than its freedom of sentiment and language, or "Death and Doctor Hornbook" from any other feeling than that of being too personal, the causes of their exclusion have remained a secret. It is less easy to account for the emission of many songs of high merit which he had among his papers: perhaps he thought those which he selected were sufficient to test the taste of the public. Before he printed the whole, he, with the consent of his brother, altered his name from Burness to Burns, a change which, I am told, he in after years regretted.

In the summer of the year 1786, the little volume, big with the hopes and fortunes of the bard made its appearance: it was entitled simply, "Poems, chiefly in the Scottish Dialect; by Robert Burns;" and accompanied by a modest preface, saying, that he submitted his book to his country with fear and with trembling, since it contained little of the art of poesie, and at the best was but a voice given, rude, he feared, and uncouth, to the loves, the hopes, and the fears of his own bosom. Had a summer sun risen on a winter morning, it could not have surprised the Lowlands of Scotland more than this Kilmarnock volume surprised and delighted the people, one and all. The milkmaid sang his songs, the ploughman repeated his poems; the old quoted both, and ever the devout rejoiced that idle verse had at last mixed a tone of morality with its mirth. The volume penetrated even into Nithsdale. "Keep it out of the way of your children," said a Cameronian divine, when he lent it to my father, "lest ye find them, as I found mine, reading it on the Sabbath." No wonder that such a volume made its way to the hearts of a peasantry whose taste in poetry had been the marvel of many writers: the poems were mostly on topics with which they were familiar: the language was that of the fireside, raised above the vulgarities of common life, by a purifying spirit of expression and the exalting fervour of inspiration: and there was such a brilliant and graceful mixture of the elegant and the homely, the lofty and the low, the familiar and the elevated — such a rapid succession of scenes which moved to tenderness or tears; or to subdued mirth or open laughter — unlooked for allusions to scripture, or touches of sarcasm and scandal — of superstitions to scare, and of humour to delight — while through the whole was diffused, as the scent of flowers through summer air, a moral meaning — a sentimental beauty, which sweetened and sanctified all. The poet's expectations from this little venture were humble: he hoped as much money from it as would pay for his passage to the West Indies, where he proposed to enter into the service of some of the Scottish settlers, and help to manage the double mystery of sugar-making and slavery.

The hearty applause which I have recorded came chiefly from the husbandman, the shepherd, and the mechanic: the approbation of the magnates of the west, though not less-warm, was longer in coming. Mrs. Stewart of Stair, indeed, commended the poems and cheered their author: Dugald Stewart received his visits with pleasure, and wondered at his vigour of conversation as much as at his muse: the door of the house of Hamilton was open to him, where the table was ever spread, and the hand ever ready to help: while the purses of the Ballantynes and the Parkers were always as open to him as were the doors of their houses. Those persons must be regarded as the real patrons of the poet: the high names of the district are not to be found among those who helped him with purse and patronage in 1786, that year of deep distress and high distinction. The Montgomerys came with their praise when his fame was up; the Kennedys and the Boswells were silent: and though the Cunninghams gave effectual aid, it was when the muse was crying with a loud voice before him, "Come all and see the man whom I delight to honour." It would be unjust as well as ungenerous not to mention the name of Mrs. Dunlop among the poet's best and early patrons: the distance at which she lived from Mossgiel had kept his name from her till his poems appeared: but his works induced her to desire his acquaintance, and she became his warmest and surest friend.

To say the truth, Burns endeavoured in every honourable way to obtain the notice of those who had influence in the land: he copied out the best of his unpublished poems in a fair hand, and inserting them in his printed volume, presented it to those who seemed slow to buy: he rewarded the notice of this one with a song — the attentions of that one with a sally of encomiastic verse: he left psalms of his own composing in the manse when he feasted with a divine: he enclosed "Holy Willie's Prayer," with an injunction to be grave, to one who loved mirth: he sent the "Holy Fair" to one whom he invited to drink a gill out of a mutchkin stoup, at Mauchline market; and on accidentally meeting with Lord Daer, he immediately commemorated the event in a sally of verse, of a strain more free and yet as flattering as ever flowed from the lips of a court bard. While musing over the names of those on whom fortune had smiled, yet who had neglected to smile on him, he remembered that he had met Miss Alexander, a young beauty of the west, in the walks of Ballochmyle; and he recorded the impression which this fair vision made on him in a song of unequalled elegance and melody. He had met her in the woods in July, on the 18th of November he sent her the song, and reminded her of the circumstance from which it arose, in a letter which it is evident he had laboured to render polished and complimentary. The young lady took no notice of either the song or the poet, though willing, it is said, to hear of both now:— this seems to have been the last attempt he made on the taste or the sympathies of the gentry of his native district: for on the very day following we find him busy in making arrangements for his departure to Jamaica.

For this step Burns had more than sufficient reasons: the profits of his volume amounted to little more than enough to waft him across the Atlantic: Wee Johnnie, though the edition was all sold, refused to risk another on speculation: his friends, both Ballantynes and Parkers, volunteered to relieve the printer's anxieties, but the poet declined their bounty, and gloomily indented himself in a ship about to sail from Greenock, and called on his muse to take farewell of Caledonia, in the last song he ever expected to measure in his native land. That fine lyric, beginning "The gloomy night is gathering fast," was the offspring of these moments of regret and sorrow. His feelings were not expressed in song alone: he remembered his mother and his natural daughter, and made an assignment of all that pertained to him at Mossgiel — and that was but little — and of all the advantage which a cruel, unjust, and insulting law allowed in the proceeds of his poems, for their support and behoof. This document was publicly read in the presence of the poet, at the market-cross of Ayr, by his friend William Chalmers, a notary public. Even this step was to Burns one of danger: some ill-advised person had uncoupled the merciless pack of the law at his heels, and he was obliged to shelter himself as he best could, in woods, it is said, by day and in barns by night,

24

till the final hour of his departure came. That hour arrived, and his chest was on the way to the ship, when a letter was put into his hand which seemed to light him to brighter prospects.

Among the friends whom his merits had procured him was Dr. Laurie, a district clergyman, who had taste enough to admire the deep sensibilities as well as the humour of the poet, and the generosity to make known both his works and his worth to the warm-hearted and amiable Blacklock, who boldly proclaimed him a poet of the first rank, and lamented that he was not in Edinburgh to publish another edition of his poems. Burns was ever a man of impulse: he recalled his chest from Greenock; he relinquished the situation he had accepted on the estate of one Douglas; took a secret leave of his mother, and, without an introduction to any one, and unknown personally to all, save to Dugald Stewart, away he walked, through Glenap, to Edinburgh, full of new hope and confiding in his genius. When he arrived, he scarcely knew what to do: he hesitated to call on the professor; he refrained from making himself known, as it has been supposed he did, to the enthusiastic Blacklock; but, sitting down in an obscure lodging, he sought out an obscure printer, recommended by a humble comrade from Kyle, and began to negotiate for a new edition of the Poems of the Ayrshire Ploughman. This was not the way to go about it: his barge had well nigh been shipwrecked in the launch; and he might have lived to regret the letter which hindered his voyage to Jamaica, had he not met by chance in the street a gentleman of the west, of the name of Dalzell, who introduced him to the Earl of Glencairn, a nobleman whose classic education did not hurt his taste for Scottish poetry, and who was not too proud to lend his helping hand to a rustic stranger of such merit as Burns. Cunningham carried him to Creech, then the Murray of Edinburgh, a shrewd man of business, who opened the poet's eyes to his true interests: the first proposals, then all but issued, were put in the fire, and new ones printed and diffused over the island. The subscription was headed by half the noblemen of the north: the Caledonian Hunt, through the interest of Glencairn, took six hundred copies: duchesses and countesses swelled the list, and such a crowding to write down names had not been witnessed since the signing of the solemn league and covenant.

While the subscription-papers were filling and the new volume printing on a paper and in a type worthy of such high patronage, Burns remained in Edinburgh, where, for the winter season, he was a lion, and one of an unwonted kind. Philosophers, historians, and scholars had shaken the elegant coteries of the city with their wit, or enlightened them with their learning, but they were all men who had been polished by polite letters or by intercourse with high life, and there was a sameness in their very dress as well as address, of which peers and peeresses had become weary. They therefore welcomed this rustic candidate for the honour of giving wings to their hours of lassitude and weariness, with a welcome more than common; and when his approach was announced, the polished circle looked for the advent of a lout from the plough, in whose uncouth manners and embarrassed address they might find matter both for mirth and wonder. But they met with a barbarian who was not at all barbarous: as the poet met in Lord Daer feelings and sentiments as natural as those of a ploughman, so they met in a ploughman manners worthy of a lord: his air was easy and unperplexed: his address was perfectly well-bred, and elegant in its simplicity: he felt neither eclipsed by the titled nor struck dumb before the learned and the eloquent, but took his station with the ease and grace of one born to it. In the society of men alone he spoke out: he spared neither his wit, his humour, nor his sarcasm — he seemed to say to all —"I am a man, and you are no more; and why should I not act and speak like one?"— it was remarked, however, that he had not learnt, or did not desire, to conceal his emotions — that he commended with more rapture than was courteous, and contradicted with more bluntness than was accounted polite. It was thus with him in the company of men: when woman approached, his look altered, his eye beamed milder; all that was stern in his nature underwent a change, and he received them with deference, but with a consciousness that he could win their attention as he had won that of others, who differed, indeed, from them only in the texture of their kirtles. This natural power of rendering himself acceptable to women had been observed and envied by Sillar, one of the dearest of his early comrades; and it stood him in good stead now, when he was the object to whom the Duchess of Gordon, the loveliest as well as the wittiest of women — directed her discourse. Burns, she afterwards said, won the attention of the Edinburgh ladies by a deferential way of address — by an ease and natural grace of manners, as new as it was unexpected — that he told them the stories of some of his tenderest songs or liveliest poems in a style quite magical — enriching his little narratives, which had one and all the merit of being short, with personal incidents of humour or of pathos.

In a party, when Dr. Blair and Professor Walker were present, Burns related the circumstances under which he had composed his melancholy song, "The gloomy night is gathering fast," in a way even more touching than the verses: and in the company of the ruling beauties of the time, he hesitated not to lift the veil from some of the tenderer parts of his own history, and give them glimpses of the romance of rustic life. A lady of birth — one of his must willing listeners — used, I am told, to say, that she should never forget the tale which he related of his affection for Mary Campbell, his Highland Mary, as he loved to call her. She was fair, he said, and affectionate, and as guileless as she was beautiful; and beautiful he thought her in a very high degree. The first time he saw her was during one of his musing walks in the woods of Montgomery Castle; and the first time he spoke to her was during the merriment of a harvest-kirn. There were others there who admired her, but he addressed her, and had the luck to win her regard from them all. He soon found that she was the lass whom he had long sought, but never before found — that her good looks were surpassed by her good sense; and her good sense was equalled by her discretion and modesty. He met her frequently: she saw by his looks that he was sincere; she put full trust in his love, and used to wander with him among the green knowes and stream-banks till the sun went down and the moon rose, talking, dreaming of love and the golden days which awaited them. He was poor, and she had only her half-year's fee, for she was in the condition of a servant; but thoughts of gear never darkened their dream: they resolved to wed, and exchanged vows of constancy and love. They plighted their vows on the Sabbath to render them more sacred — they made them by a burn, where they had courted, that open nature might be a witness — they made them over an open Bible, to show that they thought of God in this mutual act — and when they had done they both took water in their hands, and scattered it in the air, to intimate that as the stream was pure so were their intentions. They parted when they did this, but they parted never to meet more: she died in a burning fever, during a visit to her relations to prepare for her marriage; and all that he had of her was a lock of her long bright hair, and her Bible, which she exchanged for his.

Even with the tales which he related of rustic love and adventure his own story mingled; and ladies of rank heard, for the first time, that in all that was romantic in the passion of love, and in all that was chivalrous in sentiment, men of distinction, both by education and birth, were at least equalled by the peasantry of the land. They listened with interest, and inclined their feathers beside the bard, to hear how love went on in the west, and in no case it ran quite smooth. Sometimes young hearts were kept asunder by the sordid feelings of parents, who could not be persuaded to bestow their daughter, perhaps an only one, on a wooer who could not count penny for penny, and number cow for cow: sometimes a mother desired her daughter to look higher than to one of her station: for her beauty and her education entitled her to match among the lairds, rather than the tenants; and sometimes, the devotional tastes of both father and mother, approving of personal looks and connexions, were averse to see a daughter bestow her hand on one, whose language in religion was indiscreet, and whose morals were suspected. Yet, neither the vigilance of fathers, nor the suspicious care of aunts and mothers, could succeed in keeping those asunder whose hearts were together; but in these meetings circumspection and invention were necessary: all fears were to be lulled by the seeming carelessness of the lass — all perils were to be met and braved by the spirit of the lad. His home, perhaps, was at a distance, and he had wild woods to come through, and deep streams to pass, before he could see the signal-light, now shown and now withdrawn, at her window; he had to approach with a quick eye and a wary foot, lest a father or a brother should see, and deter him: he had sometimes to wish for a cloud upon the moon, whose light, welcome to him on his way in the distance, was likely to betray him when near; and he not unfrequently reckoned a wild night of wind and rain as a blessing, since it helped to conceal his coming, and proved to his mistress that he was ready to brave all for her sake. Of rivals met and baffled; of half-willing and half-unconsenting maidens, persuaded and won; of the light-hearted and the careless becoming affectionate and tender; and the coy, the proud, and the satiric being gained by "persuasive words, and more persuasive sighs," as dames had been gained of old, he had tales enow. The ladies listened, and smiled at the tender narratives of the poet.

Of his appearance among the sons as well as the daughters of men, we have the account of Dugald Stewart. "Burns," says the philosopher, "came to Edinburgh early in the winter: the attentions which he received from all ranks and descriptions of persons, were such as would have turned any head but his own. He retained the same simplicity of manners and appearance which had struck me so forcibly when I first saw him in the country: his dress was suited to his station; plain and unpretending, with sufficient attention to neatness: he always wore boots, and, when on more than usual ceremony, buckskin breeches. His manners were manly, simple, and independent; strongly expressive of conscious genius and worth, but without any indication of forwardness, arrogance, or vanity. He took his share in conversation, but not more than belonged to him, and listened with apparent deference on subjects where his want of education deprived him of the means of information. If there had been a little more of gentleness and accommodation in his temper, he would have been still more interesting; but he had been accustomed to give law in the circle of his ordinary acquaintance, and his dread of anything approaching to meanness or servility, rendered his manner somewhat decided and hard.

Nothing perhaps was more remarkable among his various attainments, than the fluency and precision and originality of language, when he spoke in company; more particularly as he aimed at purity in his turn of expression, and avoided more successfully than most Scotsmen, the peculiarities of Scottish phraseology. From his conversation I should have pronounced him to have been fitted to excel in whatever walk of ambition he had chosen to exert his abilities. He was passionately fond of the beauties of nature, and I recollect he once told me, when I was admiring a distant prospect in one of our morning walks, that the sight of so many smoking cottages gave a pleasure to his mind, which none could understand who had not witnessed, like himself, the happiness and worth which cottages contained."

Such was the impression which Burns made at first on the fair, the titled, and the learned of Edinburgh; an impression which, though lessened by intimacy and closer examination on the part of the men, remained unimpaired, on that of the softer sex, till his dying-day. His company, during the season of balls and festivities, continued to be courted by all who desired to be reckoned gay or polite. Cards of invitation fell thick on him; he was not more welcome to the plumed and jewelled groups, whom her fascinating Grace of Gordon gathered about her, than he was to the grave divines and polished scholars, who assembled in the rooms of Stewart, or Blair, or Robertson. The classic socialities of Tytler, afterwards Lord Woodhouslee, or the elaborate supper-tables of the whimsical Monboddo, whose guests imagined they were entertained in the manner of Lucullus or of Cicero, were not complete without the presence of the ploughman of Kyle; and the feelings of the rustic poet, facing such companies, though of surprise and delight at first, gradually subsided, he said, as he discerned, that man differed from man only in the polish, and not in the grain. But Edinburgh offered tables and entertainers of a less orderly and staid character than those I have named — where the glass circulated with greater rapidity; where the wit flowed more freely; and where there were neither highbred ladies to charm conversation within the bounds of modesty, nor serious philosophers, nor grave divines, to set a limit to the license of speech, or the hours of enjoyment. To these companions — and these were all of the better classes, the levities of the rustic poet's wit and humour were as welcome us were the tenderest of his narratives to the accomplished Duchess of Gordon and the beautiful Miss Burnet of Monboddo; they raised a social roar not at all classic, and demanded and provoked his sallies of wild humour, or indecorous mirth, with as much delight as he had witnessed among the lads of Kyle, when, at mill or forge, his humorous sallies abounded as the ale flowed. In these enjoyments the rough, but learned William Nicol, and the young and amiable Robert Ainslie shared: the name of the poet was coupled with those of profane wits, free livers, and that class of half-idle gentlemen who hang about the courts of law, or for a season or two wear the livery of Mars, and handle cold iron.

Edinburgh had still another class of genteel convivialists, to whom the poet was attracted by principles as well as by pleasure; these were the relics of that once numerous body, the Jacobites, who still loved to cherish the feelings of birth or education rather than of judgment, and toasted the name of Stuart, when the last of the race had renounced his pretensions to a throne, for the sake of peace and the cross. Young men then, and high names were among them, annually met on the pretender's birth-day, and sang songs in which the white rose of Jacobitism flourished; toasted toasts announcing adherence to the male line of the Bruce and the Stuart, and listened to the strains of the laureate of the day, who prophesied, in drink, the dismissal of the intrusive Hanoverian, by the right and might of the righteous and disinherited line. Burns, who was descended from a northern race, whoso father was suspected of having drawn the claymore in 1745, and who loved the blood of the Keith-Marishalls, under whose banners his ancestors had marched, readily united himself to a band in whose sentiments, political and social, he was a sharer. He was received with acclamation: the dignity of laureate was conferred upon him, and his inauguration ode, in which he recalled the names and the deeds of the Grahams, the Erskines, the Boyds, and the Gordons, was applauded for its fire, as well as for its sentiments. Yet, though he ate and drank and sang with Jacobites, he was only as far as sympathy and poesie went, of their number: his reason renounced the principles and the religion of the Stuart line; and though he shed a tear over their fallen fortunes — though he sympathized with the brave and honourable names that perished in their cause — though he cursed "the butcher, Cumberland," and the bloody spirit which commanded the heads of the good and the heroic to be stuck where they would affright the passer-by, and pollute the air — he had no desire to see the splendid fabric of constitutional freedom, which the united genius of all parties had raised, thrown wantonly down. His Jacobitism influenced, not his head, but his heart, and gave a mournful hue to many of his lyric compositions.

Meanwhile his poems were passing through the press. Burns made a few emendations of those published in the Kilmarnock edition, and he added others which, as he expressed it, he had carded and spun, since he passed Glenbuck. Some rather coarse lines were softened or omitted in the "Twa

30

Dogs;" others, from a change of his personal feelings, were made in the "Vision:" "Death and Doctor Hornbook," excluded before, was admitted now: the "Dream" was retained, in spite of the remonstrances of Mrs. Stewart, of Stair, and Mrs. Dunlop; and the "Brigs of Ayr," in compliment to his patrons in his native district, and the "Address to Edinburgh," in honour of his titled and distinguished friends in that metropolis, were printed for the first time. He was unwilling to alter what he had once printed: his friends, classic, titled, and rustic, found him stubborn and unpliable, in matters of criticism; yet he was generally of a complimental mood: he loaded the robe of Coila in the "Vision," with more scenes than it could well contain, that he might include in the landscape, all the country-seats of his friends, and he gave more than their share of commendation to the Wallaces, out of respect to his friend Mrs. Dunlop. Of the critics of Edinburgh he said, they spun the thread of their criticisms so fine that it was unfit for either warp or weft; and of its scholars, he said, they were never satisfied with any Scottish poet, unless they could trace him in Horace. One morning at Dr. Blair's breakfast-table, when the "Holy Fair" was the subject of conversation, the reverend critic said, "Why should

'—— Moody speel the holy door

With tidings of *salvation*?'

if you had said, with tidings of *damnation*, the satire would have been the better and the bitterer." "Excellent!" exclaimed the poet, "the alteration is capital, and I hope you will honour me by allowing me to say in a note at whose suggestion it was made." Professor Walker, who tells the anecdote, adds that Blair evaded, with equal good humour and decision, this not very polite request; nor was this the only slip which the poet made on this occasion: some one asked him in which of the churches of Edinburgh he had received the highest gratification: he named the High-church, but gave the preference over all preachers to Robert Walker, the colleague and rival in eloquence of Dr. Blair himself, and that in a tone so pointed and decisive as to make all at the table stare and look embarrassed. The poet confessed afterwards that he never reflected on his blunder without pain and mortification. Blair probably had this in his mind, when, on reading the poem beginning "When Guildford good our pilot stood," he exclaimed, "Ah! the politics of Burns always smell of the smithy," meaning, that they were vulgar and common.

In April, the second or Edinburgh, edition was published: it was widely purchased, and as warmly commended. The country had been prepared for it by the generous and discriminating criticisms of Henry Mackenzie, published in that popular periodical, "The Lounger," where he says, "Burns possesses the spirit as well as the fancy of a poet; that honest pride and independence of soul, which are sometimes the muse's only dower, break forth on every occasion, in his works." The praise of the author of the "Man of Feeling" was not more felt by Burns, than it was by the whole island: the harp of the north had not been swept for centuries by a hand so forcible, and at the same time so varied, that it awakened every tone, whether of joy or woe: the language was that of rustic life; the scenes of the poems were the dusty barn, the clay-floored reeky cottage, and the furrowed field; and the characters were cowherds, ploughmen, and mechanics. The volume was embellished by a head of the poet from the hand of the now venerable Alexander Nasmith; and introduced by a dedication to the noblemen and gentlemen of the Caledonian Hunt, in a style of vehement independence, unknown hitherto in the history of subscriptions. The whole work, verse, prose, and portrait, won public attention, and kept it: and though some critics signified their displeasure at expressions which bordered on profanity, and at a license of language which they pronounced impure, by far the greater number united their praise to the all but general voice; nay, some scrupled not to call him, from his perfect ease and nature and variety, the Scottish Shakspeare. No one rejoiced more in his success and his fame, than the matron of Mossgiel.

Other matters than his poems and socialities claimed the attention of Burns in Edinburgh. He had a hearty relish for the joyous genius of Allan Ramsay; he traced out his residences, and rejoiced to think that while he stood in the shop of his own bookseller, Creech, the same floor had been trod by the feet of his great forerunner. He visited, too, the lowly grave of the unfortunate Robert Fergusson; and it must be recorded to the shame of the magistrates of Edinburgh, that they allowed him to erect a headstone to his memory, and to the scandal of Scotland, that in such a memorial he had not been anticipated. He seems not to have regarded the graves of scholars or philosophers; and he trod the pavements where the warlike princes and nobles had walked without any emotion. He loved, however, to see places celebrated in Scottish song, and fields where battles for the independence of his country had been stricken; and, with money in his pocket which his poems had produced, and with a letter from a witty but weak man, Lord Buchan, instructing him to pull birks on the Yarrow, broom on the Cowden-knowes, and not to neglect to admire the ruins of Drybrugh Abbey, Burns set out on a border tour, accompanied by Robert Ainslie, of Berrywell. As the poet had talked of returning to the plough, Dr. Blair imagined that he was on his way back to the furrowed field, and wrote him a handsome farewell, saying he was leaving Edinburgh with a character which had survived many temptations; with a name which would be placed with the Ramsays and the Fergussons, and with the hopes of all, that, in a second volume, on which his fate as a poet would very much depend, he might rise yet higher in merit and in fame. Burns, who received this communication when laying his leg over the saddle to be gone, is said to have muttered, "Ay, but a man's first book is sometimes like his first babe, healthier and stronger than those which follow."

On the 6th of May, 1787, Burns reached Berrywell: he recorded of the laird, that he was clear-headed, and of Miss Ainslie, that she was amiable and handsome — of Dudgeon, the author of "The Maid that tends the Goats," that he had penetration and modesty, and of the preacher, Bowmaker, that he was a man of strong lungs and vigorous remark. On crossing the Tweed at Coldstream he took off his hat, and kneeling down, repeated aloud the two last verses of the "Cotter's Saturday Night:" on returning, he drunk tea with Brydone, the traveller, a man, he said, kind and benevolent: he cursed one Cole as an English Hottentot, for having rooted out an ancient garden belonging to a Romish ruin; and he wrote of Macdowal, of Caverton-mill, that by his skill in rearing sheep, he sold his flocks, ewe and lamb, for a couple of guineas each: that he washed his sheep before shearing — and by his turnips improved sheep-husbandry; he added, that lands were generally let at sixteen shillings the Scottish acre; the farmers rich, and, compared to Ayrshire, their houses magnificent. On his way to Jedburgh he visited an old gentleman in whose house was an arm-chair, once the property of the author of "The Seasons;" he reverently examined the relic, and could scarcely be persuaded to sit in it: he was a warm admirer of Thomson.

In Jedburgh, Burns found much to interest him: the ruins of a splendid cathedral, and of a strong castle — and, what was still more attractive, an amiable young lady, very handsome, with "beautiful hazel eyes, full of spirit, sparkling with delicious moisture," and looks which betokened a high order of female mind. He gave her his portrait, and entered this remembrance of her attractions among his memoranda:—"My heart is thawed into melting pleasure, after being so long frozen up in the Greenland bay of indifference, amid the noise and nonsense of Edinburgh. I am afraid my bosom has nearly as much tinder as ever. Jed, pure be thy streams, and hallowed thy sylvan banks: sweet Isabella Lindsay, may peace dwell in thy bosom uninterrupted, except by the tumultuous throbbings of rapturous love!" With the freedom of Jedburgh, handsomely bestowed by the magistrates, in his pocket, Burns made his way to Wauchope, the residence of Mrs. Scott, who had welcomed him into the world as a poet in verses lively and graceful: he found her, he said, "a lady of sense and taste, and of a decision peculiar to female authors." After dining with Sir Alexander Don, who, he said, was a clever man, but far from a match for his divine lady, a sister of his patron Glencairn, he spent an hour among the beautiful ruins of Dryburgh Abbey; glanced on the splendid remains of Melrose; passed, unconscious of the future, over that ground on which have arisen the romantic towers of Abbotsford; dined with certain of the Souters of Selkirk; and visited the old keep of Thomas the Rhymer, and a dozen of the hills and streams celebrated in song. Nor did he fail to pay his respects, after returning through Dunse, to Sir James Hall, of Dunglass, and his lady, and was much pleased with the scenery of their romantic place. He was now joined by a gentleman of the name of Kerr, and crossing the Tweed a second time, penetrated into England, as far as the ancient town of Newcastle, where he smiled at a facetious Northumbrian, who at dinner caused the beef to be eaten before the broth was served, in obedience to an ancient injunction, lest the hungry Scotch should come and snatch it. On his way back he saw, what proved to be prophetic of his own fortune — the roup of an unfortunate farmer's stock: he took out his journal, and wrote with a troubled brow, "Rigid economy, and decent industry, do you preserve me from being the principal *dramatis personæ*, in such a scene of horror." He extended his tour to Carlisle, and from thence to the banks of the Nith, where he looked at the farm of Ellisland, with the intention of trying once more his fortune at the plough, should poetry and patronage fail him.

On his way through the West, Burns spent a few days with his mother at Mossgiel: he had left her an unknown and an almost banished man: he returned in fame and in sunshine, admired by all who aspired to be thought tasteful or refined. He felt offended alike with the patrician stateliness of Edinburgh and the plebeian servility of the husbandmen of Ayrshire; and dreading the influence of the unlucky star which had hitherto ruled his lot, he bought a pocket Milton, he said, for the purpose of studying the intrepid independence and daring magnanimity, and noble defiance of hardships, exhibited by Satan! In this mood he reached Edinburgh — only to leave it again on three hurried excursions into the Highlands. The route which he took and the sentiments which the scenes awakened, are but faintly intimated in the memoranda which he made. His first journey seems to have been performed in ill-humour; at Stirling, his Jacobitism, provoked at seeing the ruined palace of the Stuarts, broke out in some unloyal lines which he had the indiscretion to write with a diamond on the window of a public inn. At Carron, where he was refused a sight of the magnificent foundry, he avenged himself in epigram. At Inverary he resented some real or imaginary neglect on the part of his Grace of Argyll, by a stinging lampoon; nor can he be said to have fairly regained his serenity of temper, till he danced his wrath away with some Highland ladies at Dumbarton.

His second excursion was made in the company of Dr. Adair, of Harrowgate: the reluctant doors of Carron foundry were opened to him, and he expressed his wonder at the blazing furnaces and broiling labours of the place; he removed the disloyal lines from the window of the inn at Stirling, and he paid a two days' visit to Ramsay of Ochtertyre, a distinguished scholar, and discussed with him future topics for the muse. "I have been in the company of many men of genius," said Ramsay afterwards to Currie, "some of them poets, but never witnessed such flashes of intellectual brightness as from him — the impulse of the moment, sparks of celestial fire." From the Forth he went to the Devon, in the county of Clackmannan, where, for the first time, he saw the beautiful Charlotte Hamilton, the sister of his friend Gavin Hamilton, of Mauchline. "She is not only beautiful," he thus writes to her brother, "but lovely: her form is elegant, her features not regular, but they have the smile of sweetness, and the settled complacency of good nature in the highest degree. Her eyes are fascinating; at once expressive of good sense, tenderness and a noble mind. After the exercise of our riding to the Falls, Charlotte was exactly Dr. Donne's mistress:—

"Her pure and eloquent blood

Spoke in her cheeks, and so distinctly wrought,

That one would almost say her body thought."

Accompanied by this charming dame, he visited an old lady, Mrs. Bruce, of Clackmannan, who, in the belief that she had the blood of the royal Bruce in her veins, received the poet with something of princely state, and, half in jest, conferred the honour of knighthood upon him, with her ancestor's sword, saying, in true Jacobitical mood, that she had a better right to do that than some folk had! In the same pleasing company he visited the famous cataract on the Devon, called the Cauldron Lian, and the Rumbling bridge, a single arch thrown, it is said by the devil, over the

35

Devon, at the height of a hundred feet in the air. It was the complaint of his companions that Burns exhibited no raptures, and poured out no unpremeditated verses at such magnificent scenes. But he did not like to be tutored or prompted: "Look, look!" exclaimed some one, as Carron foundry belched forth flames —"look, Burns, look! good heavens, what a grand sight! — look!" "I would not look — look, sir, at your bidding," said the bard, turning away, "were it into the mouth of hell!" When he visited, at a future time, the romantic Linn of Creehope, in Nithsdale, he looked silently at its wonders, and showed none of the hoped-for rapture. "You do not admire it, I fear," said a gentleman who accompanied him; "I could not admire it more, sir," replied Burns, "if He who made it were to desire me to do it." There are other reasons for the silence of Burns amid the scenes of the Devon: he was charmed into love by the sense and the beauty of Charlotte Hamilton, and rendered her homage in that sweet song, "The Banks of the Devon," and in a dozen letters written with more than his usual care, elegance, and tenderness. But the lady was neither to be won by verse nor by prose: she afterwards gave her hand to Adair, the poet's companion, and, what was less meritorious, threw his letters into the fire.

The third and last tour into the North was in company of Nicol of the High-School of Edinburgh: on the fields of Bannockburn and Falkirk — places of triumph and of woe to Scotland, he gave way to patriotic impulses, and in these words he recorded them:—"Stirling, August 20, 1787: this morning I knelt at the tomb of Sir John the Graham, the gallant friend of the immortal Wallace; and two hours ago I said a fervent prayer for old Caledonia, over the hole in a whinstone where Robert the Bruce fixed his royal standard on the banks of Bannockburn." He then proceeded northward by Ochtertyre, the water of Earn, the vale of Glen Almond, and the traditionary grave of Ossian. He looked in at princely Taymouth; mused an hour or two among the Birks of Aberfeldy; gazed from Birnam top; paused amid the wild grandeur of the pass of Killiecrankie, at the stone which marks the spot where a second patriot Graham fell, and spent a day at Blair, where he experienced the graceful kindness of the Duke of Athol, and in a strain truly elegant, petitioned him, in the name of Bruar Water, to hide the utter nakedness of its otherwise picturesque banks, with plantations of birch and oak. Quitting Blair he followed the course of the Spey, and passing, as he told his brother, through a wild country, among cliffs gray with eternal snows, and glens gloomy and savage, reached Findhorn in mist and darkness; visited Castle Cawdor, where Macbeth murdered Duncan; hastened through Inverness to Urquhart Castle, and the Falls of Fyers, and turned southward to Kilravock, over the fatal moor of Culloden. He admired the ladies of that classic region for their snooded ringlets, simple elegance of dress, and expressive eyes: in Mrs. Rose, of Kilravock Castle, he found that matronly grace and dignity which he owned he loved; and in the Duke and Duchess of Gordon a renewal of that more than kindness with which they had welcomed him in Edinburgh. But while he admired the palace of Fochabers, and was charmed by the condescensions of the noble proprietors, he forgot that he had left a companion at the inn, too proud and captious to be pleased at favours showered on others: he hastened back to the inn with an invitation and an apology: he found the fiery pedant in a foaming rage, striding up and down the street, cursing in Scotch and Latin the loitering postilions for not yoking the horses, and hurrying him away. All apology and explanation was in vain, and Burns, with a vexation which he sought not to conceal, took his seat silently beside the irascible pedagogue, and returned to the South by Broughty Castle, the banks of Endermay and Queensferry. He parted with the Highlands in a kindly mood, and loved to recal the scenes and the people, both in conversation and in song.

On his return to Edinburgh he had to bide the time of his bookseller and the public: the impression of his poems, extending to two thousand eight hundred copies, was sold widely: much of the money had to come from a distance, and Burns lingered about the northern metropolis, expecting a settlement with Creech, and with the hope that those who dispensed his country's patronage might remember one who then, as now, was reckoned an ornament to the land. But Creech, a parsimonious man, was slow in his payments; the patronage of the country was swallowed up in the sink of politics, and though noblemen smiled, and ladies of rank nodded their jewelled heads in approbation of every new song he sung and every witty sally he uttered, they reckoned any further notice or care superfluous: the poet, an observant man, saw all this; but hope was the cordial of his heart, he said, and he hoped and lingered on. Too active a genius to remain idle, he addressed himself to the twofold business of love and verse. Repulsed by the stately Beauty of the Devon, he sought consolation in the society of one, as fair, and infinitely more witty; and as an accident had for a time deprived him of the use of one of his legs, he gave wings to hours of pain, by writing a series of letters to this Edinburgh enchantress, in which he signed himself Sylvander, and addressed her under the name of Clarinda. In these compositions, which no one can regard as serious, and which James Grahame the poet called "a romance of real Platonic affection," amid much affectation both of language and sentiment, and a desire to say fine and startling things, we can see the proud heart of the poet throbbing in the dread of being neglected or forgotten by his country. The love which he offers up at the altar of wit and beauty, seems assumed and put on, for its rapture is artificial, and its brilliancy that of an icicle: no woman was ever wooed and won in that Malvolio way; and there is no doubt that Mrs. M'Lehose felt as much offence as pleasure at this boisterous display of regard. In aftertimes he loved to remember her:— when wine circulated, Mrs. Mac was his favourite toast.

During this season he began his lyric contributions to the Musical Museum of Johnson, a work which, amid many imperfections of taste and arrangement, contains more of the true old music and genuine old songs of Scotland, than any other collection with which I am acquainted. Burns gathered oral airs, and fitted them with words of mirth or of woe, of tenderness or of humour, with unexampled readiness and felicity; he eked out old fragments and sobered down licentious strains so much in the olden spirit and feeling, that the new cannot be distinguished from the ancient; nay, he inserted lines and half lines, with such skill and nicety, that antiquarians are perplexed to settle which is genuine or which is simulated. Yet with all this he abated not of the natural mirth or the racy humour of the lyric muse of Scotland: he did not like her the less because she walked like some of the maidens of her strains, high-kilted at times, and spoke with the freedom of innocence. In these communications we observe how little his border-jaunt among the fountains of ancient song contributed either of sentiment or allusion, to his lyrics; and how deeply his strains, whether of pity or of merriment, were coloured by what he had seen, and heard, and felt in the Highlands. In truth, all that lay beyond the Forth was an undiscovered land to him; while the lowland districts were not only familiar to his mind and eye, but all their more romantic vales and hills and streams were already musical in songs of such excellence as induced him to dread failure rather than hope triumph. Moreover, the Highlands teemed with jacobitical feelings, and scenes hallowed by the blood or the sufferings of men heroic, and perhaps misguided; and the poet, willingly yielding to an impulse which was truly romantic, and believed by thousands to be loyal, penned his songs on Drumossie, and Killiecrankie, as the spirit of sorrow or of bitterness prevailed. Though accompanied, during his northern excursions, by friends whose socialities and conversation forbade deep thought, or even serious remark, it will be seen by those who read his lyrics with care, that his wreath is indebted for some of its fairest flowers to the Highlands.

The second winter of the poet's abode in Edinburgh had now arrived: it opened, as might have been expected, with less rapturous welcomes and with more of frosty civility than the first. It must be confessed, that indulgence in prolonged socialities, and in company which, though clever, could not be called select, contributed to this; nor must it be forgotten that his love for the sweeter part of creation was now and then carried beyond the limits of poetic respect, and the delicacies of courtesy; tending to estrange the austere and to lessen the admiration at first common to all. Other causes may be assigned for this wane of popularity: he took no care to conceal his contempt for all who depended on mere scholarship for eminence, and he had a perilous knack in sketching with a sarcastic hand the characters of the learned and the grave. Some indeed of the high literati of the north — Home, the author of Douglas, was one of them — spoke of the poet as a chance or an accident: and though they admitted that he was a poet, yet he was not one of settled grandeur of soul, brightened by study. Burns was probably aware of this; he takes occasion in some of his letters to suggest, that the hour may be at hand when he shall be accounted by scholars as a meteor, rather than a fixed light, and to suspect that the praise bestowed on his genius was partly owing to the humility of his condition. From his lingering so long about Edinburgh, the nobility began to dread a second volume by subscription, the learned to regard him as a fierce Theban, who resolved to carry all the outworks to the temple of Fame without the labour of making regular approaches; while a third party, and not the least numerous, looked on him with distrust, as one who hovered between Jacobite and Jacobin; who disliked the loyal-minded, and loved to lampoon the reigning family. Besides, the marvel of the inspired ploughman had begun to subside; the bright gloss of novelty was worn off, and his fault lay in his unwillingness to see that he had made all the sport which the Philistines expected, and was required to make room for some "salvage" of the season, to paw, and roar, and shake the mane. The doors of the titled, which at first opened spontaneous, like those in Milton's heaven, were now unclosed for him with a tardy courtesy: he was received with measured stateliness, and seldom requested to repeat his visit. Of this changed aspect of things he complained to a friend: but his real sorrows were mixed with those of the fancy:— he told Mrs. Dunlop with what pangs of heart he was compelled to take shelter in a corner, lest the rattling equipage of some gaping blockhead should mangle him in the mire. In this land of titles and wealth such querulous sensibilities must have been frequently offended.

Burns, who had talked lightly hitherto of resuming the plough, began now to think seriously about it, for he saw it must come to that at last. Miller, of Dalswinton, a gentleman of scientific acquirements, and who has the merit of applying the impulse of steam to navigation, had offered the poet the choice of his farms, on a fair estate which he had purchased on the Nith: aided by a westland farmer, he selected Ellisland, a beautiful spot, fit alike for the steps of ploughman or poet. On intimating this to the magnates of Edinburgh, no one lamented that a genius so bright and original should be driven to win his bread with the sweat of his brow: no one, with an indignant eye, ventured to tell those to whom the patronage of this magnificent empire was confided, that they were misusing the sacred trust, and that posterity would curse them for their coldness or neglect: neither did any of the rich nobles, whose tables he had adorned by his wit, offer to enable him to toil free of rent, in a land of which he was to be a permanent ornament; — all were silent — all were cold — the Earl of Glencairn alone, aided by Alexander Wood, a gentleman who merits praise oftener than he is named, did the little that was done or attempted to be done for him: nor was that little done on the peer's part without solicitation:—"I wish to go into the excise;" thus he wrote to Glencairn; "and I am told your lordship's interest will easily procure me the grant from the commissioners: and your lordship's patronage and goodness, which have already rescued me from obscurity, wretchedness, and exile, emboldens me to ask that interest. You have likewise put it in my power to save the little tie of home that sheltered an aged mother, two brothers, and three sisters from destruction. I am ill qualified to dog the heels of greatness with the impertinence of solicitation, and tremble nearly as much at the thought of the cold promise as the cold denial." The farm and the excise exhibit the poet's humble scheme of life: the money of the one, he thought, would support the toil of the other, and in the fortunate management of both, he looked for the rough abundance, if not the elegancies suitable to a poet's condition.

While Scotland was disgraced by sordidly allowing her brightest genius to descend to the plough and the excise, the poet hastened his departure from a city which had witnessed both his triumph and his shame: he bade farewell in a few well-chosen words to such of the classic literati — the Blairs, the Stewarts, the Mackenzies, and the Tytlers — as had welcomed the rustic bard and continued to countenance him; while in softer accents he bade adieu to the Clarindas and Chlorises of whose charms he had sung, and, having wrung a settlement from Creech, he turned his steps towards Mossgiel and Mauchline. He had several reasons, and all serious ones, for taking Ayrshire in his way to the Nith: he desired to see his mother, his brothers and sisters, who had partaken of his success, and were now raised from pining penury to comparative affluence: he desired to see those who had aided him in his early struggles into the upper air — perhaps those, too, who had looked coldly on, and smiled at his outward aspirations after fame or distinction; but more than all, he desired to see one whom he once and still dearly loved, who had been a sufferer for his sake, and whom he proposed to make mistress of his fireside and the sharer of his fortunes. Even while whispering of love to Charlotte Hamilton, on the banks of the Devon, or sighing out the affected sentimentalities of platonic or pastoral love in the ear of Clarinda, his thoughts wandered to her whom he had left bleaching her webs among the daisies on Mauchline braes — she had still his heart, and in spite of her own and her father's disclamation, she was his wife. It was one of the delusions of this great poet, as well as of those good people, the Armours, that the marriage had been dissolved by the destruction of the marriage-lines, and that Robert Burns and Jean Armour were as single as though they had neither vowed nor written themselves man and wife. Be that as it may, the time was come when all scruples and obstacles were to be removed which stood in the way of their union: their hands were united by Gavin Hamilton, according to law, in April, 1788: and even the Reverend Mr. Auld, so mercilessly lampooned, smiled forgivingly as the poet satisfied a church wisely scrupulous regarding the sacred ceremony of marriage.

Though Jean Armour was but a country lass of humble degree, she had sense and intelligence, and personal charms sufficient not only to win and fix the attentions of the poet, but to sanction the praise which he showered on her in song. In a letter to Mrs. Dunlop, he thus describes her: "The most placid good nature and sweetness of disposition, a warm heart, gratefully devoted with all its powers to love me; vigorous health and sprightly cheerfulness, set off to the best advantage by a more than commonly handsome figure: these I think in a woman may make a good wife, though she should never have read a page but the Scriptures, nor have danced in a brighter assembly than a penny-pay wedding." To the accomplished Margaret Chalmers, of Edinburgh, he adds, to complete the picture, "I have got the handsomest figure, the sweetest temper, the soundest constitution, and kindest heart in the country: a certain late publication of Scots' poems she has perused very devoutly, and all the ballads in the land, as she has the finest wood-note wild you ever heard." With his young wife, a punch bowl of Scottish marble, and an eight-day clock, both presents from Mr. Armour, now reconciled to his eminent son-in-law, with a new plough, and a beautiful heifer, given by Mrs. Dunlop, with about four hundred pounds in his pocket, a resolution to toil, and a hope of success, Burns made his appearance on the banks of the Nith, and set up his staff at Ellisland. This farm, now a classic spot, is about six miles up the river from Dumfries; it extends to upwards of a hundred acres: the soil is kindly; the holmland portion of it loamy and rich, and it has at command fine walks on the river side, and views of the Friar's Carse, Cowehill, and Dalswinton. For a while the poet had to hide his head in a smoky hovel; till a house to his fancy, and offices for his cattle and his crops were built, his accommodation was sufficiently humble; and his mind taking its hue from his situation, infused a bitterness into the letters in which he first made known to his western friends that he had fixed his abode in Nithsdale. "I am here," said he, "at the very elbow of existence: the only things to be found in perfection in this country are stupidity and canting; prose they only know in graces and prayers, and the value of these they estimate as they do their plaiden-webs, by the ell: as for the muses, they have as much an idea of a rhinoceros as of a poet." "This is an undiscovered clime," he at another period exclaims, "it is unknown to poetry, and prose never looked on it save in drink. I sit by the fire, and listen to the hum of the spinning-wheel: I hear, but cannot see it, for it is hidden in the smoke which eddies round and round me before it seeks to escape by window and door. I have no converse but with the ignorance which encloses me: No kenned face but that of my old mare, Jenny Geddes — my life is dwindled down to mere existence."

When the poet's new house was built and plenished, and the atmosphere of his mind began to clear, he found the land to be fruitful, and its people intelligent and wise. In Riddel, of Friar's Carse, he found a scholar and antiquarian; in Miller, of Dalswinton, a man conversant with science as well as with the world; in M'Murdo, of Drumlanrig, a generous and accomplished gentleman; and in John Syme, of Ryedale, a man much after his own heart, and a lover of the wit and socialities of polished life. Of these gentlemen Riddel, who was his neighbour, was the favourite: a door was made in the march-fence which separated Ellisland from Friar's Carse, that the poet might indulge in the retirement of the Carse hermitage, a little lodge in the wood, as romantic as it was beautiful, while a pathway was cut through the dwarf oaks and birches which fringed the river bank, to enable the poet to saunter and muse without lot or interruption. This attention was rewarded by an inscription for the hermitage, written with elegance as well as feeling, and which was the first fruits of his fancy in this unpoetic land. In a happier strain he remembered Matthew Henderson: this is one of the sweetest as well as happiest of his poetic compositions. He heard of his friend's death, and called on nature animate and inanimate, to lament the loss of one who held the patent of his honours from God alone, and who loved all that was pure and lovely and good. "The Whistle" is another of his Ellisland compositions: the contest which he has recorded with such spirit and humour took place almost at his door: the heroes were Fergusson, of Craigdarroch, Sir Robert Laurie, of Maxwelltown, and Riddel, of the Friar's Carse: the poet was present, and drank bottle and bottle about with the best, and when all was done he seemed much disposed, as an old servant at Friar's Carse remembered, to take up the victor.

Burns had become fully reconciled to Nithsdale, and was on the most intimate terms with the muse when he produced Tam O' Shanter, the crowning glory of all his poems. For this marvellous tale we are indebted to something like accident: Francis Grose, the antiquary, happened to visit Friar's Carse, and as he loved wine and wit, the total want of imagination was no hinderance to his friendly intercourse with the poet: "Alloway's auld haunted kirk" was mentioned, and Grose said he would include it in his illustrations of the antiquities of Scotland, if the bard of the Doon would write a poem to accompany it. Burns consented, and before he left the table, the various traditions which belonged to the ruin were passing through his mind. One of these was of a farmer, who, on a night wild with wind and rain, on passing the old kirk was startled by a light glimmering inside the walls; on drawing near he saw a caldron hung over a fire, in which the heads and limbs of children were simmering: there was neither witch nor fiend to guard it, so he unhooked the caldron, turned out the contents, and carried it home as a trophy. A second tradition was of a man of Kyle, who, having been on a market night detained late in Ayr, on crossing the old bridge of Doon, on his way home, saw a light streaming through the gothic window of Alloway kirk, and on riding near, beheld a batch of the district witches dancing merrily round their master, the devil, who kept them "louping and flinging" to the sound of a bagpipe. He knew several of the old crones, and smiled at their gambols, for they were dancing in their smocks: but one of them, and she happened to be young and rosy, had on a smock shorter than those of her companions by two spans at least, which so moved the farmer that he exclaimed, "Weel luppan, Maggie wi' the short sark!" Satan stopped his music, the light was extinguished, and out rushed the hags after the farmer, who made at the gallop for the bridge of Doon, knowing that they could not cross a stream: he escaped; but Maggie, who was foremost, seized his horse's tail at the middle of the bridge, and pulled it off in her efforts to stay him.

This poem was the work of a single day: Burns walked out to his favourite musing path, which runs towards the old tower of the Isle, along

43

Nithside, and was observed to walk hastily and mutter as he went. His wife knew by these signs that he was engaged in composition, and watched him from the window; at last wearying, and moreover wondering at the unusual length of his meditations, she took her children with her and went to meet him; but as he seemed not to see her, she stept aside among the broom to allow him to pass, which he did with a flushed brow and dropping eyes, reciting these lines aloud:—

"Now Tam! O, Tum! had thae been queans,

A' plump and strapping in their teens,

Their sacks, instead o' creeshie flannen,

Been snaw-white seventeen hunder linen!

Thir breeks o' mine, my only pair,

That ance were plush, o' gude blue hair,

I wad hae gien them off my hurdies,

For ae blink o' the bonnie burdies!"

He embellished this wild tradition from fact as well as from fancy: along the road which Tam came on that eventful night his memory supplied circumstances which prepared him for the strange sight at the kirk of Alloway. A poor chapman had perished, some winters before, in the snow; a murdered child had been found by some early hunters; a tippling farmer had fallen from his horse at the expense of his neck, beside a "meikle stane"; and a melancholy old woman had hanged herself at the bush aboon the well, as the poem relates: all these matters the poet pressed into the service of the muse, and used them with a skill which adorns rather than oppresses the legend. A pert lawyer from Dumfries objected to the language as obscure: "Obscure, sir!" said Burns; "you know not the language of that great master of your own art — the devil. If you had a witch for your client you would not be able to manage her defence!"

He wrote few poems after his marriage, but he composed many songs: the sweet voice of Mrs. Burns and the craving of Johnson's Museum will in some measure account for the number, but not for their variety, which is truly wonderful. In the history of that mournful strain, "Mary in Heaven," we read the story of many of his lyrics, for they generally sprang from his personal feelings: no poet has put more of himself into his poetry than Burns, "Robert, though ill of a cold," said his wife, "had been busy all day — a day of September, 1789, with the shearers in the field, and as he had got most of the corn into the stack-yard, was in good spirits; but when twilight came he grew sad about something, and could not rest: he wandered first up the waterside, and then went into the stack-yard: I followed, and begged him to come into the house, as he was ill, and the air was sharp and cold. He said, 'Ay, ay,' but did not come: he threw himself down on some loose sheaves, and lay looking at the sky, and particularly at a large, bright star, which shone like another moon. At last, but that was long after I had left him, he came home — the song was already composed." To the memory of Mary Campbell he dedicated that touching ode; and he thus intimates the continuance of his early affection for "The fair haired lass of the west," in a letter of that time to Mrs. Dunlop. "If there is another life, it must be only for the just, the benevolent, the amiable, and the humane. What a flattering idea, then, is a world to come! There shall I, with speechless agony of rapture, again recognise my lost, my ever dear Mary, whose bosom was fraught with truth, honour, constancy, and love." These melancholy words gave way in their turn to others of a nature lively and humorous: "Tam Glen," in which the thoughts flow as freely as the waters of the Nith, on whose banks he wrote it; "Findlay," with its quiet vein of sly simplicity; "Willie brewed a peck o' maut," the first of social, and "She's fair and fause," the first of sarcastic songs, with "The deil's awa wi' the Exciseman," are all productions of this period — a period which had besides its own fears and its own forebodings.

For a while Burns seemed to prosper in his farm: he held the plough with his own hand, he guided the harrows, he distributed the seed-corn equally among the furrows, and he reaped the crop in its season, and saw it safely covered in from the storms of winter with "thack and rape;" his wife, too, superintended the dairy with a skill which she had brought from Kyle, and as the harvest, for a season or two, was abundant, and the dairy yielded butter and cheese for the market, it seemed that "the luckless star" which ruled his lot had relented, and now shone unboding and benignly. But much more is required than toil of hand to make a successful farmer, nor will the attention bestowed only by fits and starts, compensate for carelessness or oversight: frugality, not in one thing but in all, is demanded, in small matters as well as in great, while a careful mind and a vigilant eye must superintend the labours of servants, and the whole system of in-door and out-door economy. Now, during the three years which Burns stayed in Ellisland, he neither wrought with that constant diligence which farming demands, nor did he bestow upon it the unremitting attention of eye and mind which such a farm required: besides his skill in husbandry was but moderate — the rent, though of his own fixing, was too high for him and for the times; the ground, though good, was not so excellent as he might have had on the same estate — he employed more servants than the number of acres demanded, and spread for them a richer board than common: when we have said this we need not add the expensive tastes induced by poetry, to keep readers from starting, when they are told that Burns, at the close of the third year of occupation, resigned his lease to the landlord, and bade farewell for ever to the plough. He was not, however, quite desolate; he had for a year or more been appointed on the excise, and had superintended a district extending to ten large parishes, with applause; indeed, it has been assigned as the chief reason for failure in his farm, that when the plough or the sickle summoned him to the field, he was to be found, either pursuing the defaulters of the revenue, among the valleys of Dumfrieshire, or measuring out pastoral verse to the beauties of the land. He retired to a house in the Bank-vennel of Dumfries, and commenced a town-life: he commenced it with an empty pocket, for Ellisland had swallowed up all the profits of his poems: he had now neither a barn to produce meal nor barley, a barn-yard to yield a fat hen, a field to which he could go at Martinmas for a mart, nor a dairy to supply milk and cheese and butter to the table — he had, in short, all to buy and little to buy with. He regarded it as a compensation that he had no farm-rent to provide, no bankruptcies to dread, no horse to keep, for his excise duties were now confined to Dumfries, and that the burthen of a barren farm was removed from his mind, and his muse at liberty to renew her unsolicited strains.

But from the day of his departure from "the barren" Ellisland, the downward course of Burns may be dated. The cold neglect of his country had driven him back indignantly to the plough, and he hoped to gain from the furrowed field that independence which it was the duty of Scotland to have provided: but he did not resume the plough with all the advantages he possessed when he first forsook it: he had revelled in the luxuries of polished life — his tastes had been rendered expensive as well as pure: he had witnessed, and he hoped for the pleasures of literary retirement, while the hands which had led jewelled dames over scented carpets to supper tables leaded with silver took hold of the hilts of the plough with more of reluctance than good-will. Edinburgh, with its lords and its ladies, its delights and its hopes, spoiled him for farming. Nor were his new labours more acceptable to his haughty spirit than those of the plough: the excise for a century had been a word of opprobrium or of hatred in the north: the duties which it imposed were regarded, not by peasants alone, as a serious encroachment upon the ancient rights of the nation, and to mislead a gauger, or resist him, even to blood, was considered by few as a fault. That the brightest genius of the nation — one whose tastes and sensibilities were so peculiarly its own — should be, as a reward, set to look after run-rum and smuggled tobacco, and to gauge ale-wife's barrels, was a regret and a marvel to many, and a source of bitter merriment to Burns himself.

The duties of his situation were however performed punctually, if not with pleasure: he was a vigilant officer; he was also a merciful and considerate one: though loving a joke, and not at all averse to a dram, he walked among suspicious brewers, captious ale-wives, and frowning shop-keepers as uprightly as courteously: he smoothed the ruggedest natures into acquiescence by his gayety and humour, and yet never gave cause for a malicious remark, by allowing his vigilance to slumber. He was brave, too, and in the capture of an armed smuggler, in which he led the attack, showed that he neither feared water nor fire: he loved, also, to counsel the more forward of the smugglers to abandon their dangerous calling; his sympathy for the helpless poor induced him to give them now and then notice of his approach; he has been known to interpret the severe laws of the excise into tenderness and mercy in behalf of the widow and the fatherless. In all this he did but his duty to his country and his kind: and his conduct was so regarded by a very competent and candid judge. "Let me look at the books of Burns," said Maxwell, of Terraughty, at the meeting of the district magistrates, "for they show that an upright officer may be a merciful one." With a salary of some seventy pounds a year, the chance of a few guineas annually from the future editions of his poems, and the hope of rising at some distant day to the more lucrative situation of supervisor, Burns continued to live in Dumfries; first in the Bank-vennel, and next in a small house in a humble street, since called by his name.

In his earlier years the poet seems to have scattered songs as thick as a summer eve scatters its dews; nor did he scatter them less carelessly: he appears, indeed, to have thought much less of them than of his poems: the sweet song of Mary Morison, and others not at all inferior, lay unregarded among his papers till accident called them out to shine and be admired.

Many of these brief but happy compositions, sometimes with his name, and oftener without, he threw in dozens at a time into Johnson, where they were noticed only by the captious Ritson: but now a work of higher pretence claimed a share in his skill: in September, 1792, he was requested by George Thomson to render, for his national collection, the poetry worthy of the muses of the north, and to take compassion on many choice airs, which had waited for a poet like the author of the Cotter's Saturday Night, to wed them to immortal verse. To engage in such an undertaking, Burns required small persuasion, and while Thomson asked for strains delicate and polished, the poet characteristically stipulated that his contributions were to be without remuneration, and the language seasoned with a sprinkling of the Scottish dialect. As his heart was much in the matter, he began to pour out verse with a readiness and talent unknown in the history of song: his engagement with Thomson, and his esteem for Johnson, gave birth to a series of songs as brilliant as varied, and as naturally easy as they were gracefully original. In looking over those very dissimilar collections it is not difficult to discover that the songs which he wrote for the more stately work, while they are more polished and elegant than those which he contributed to the less pretending one, are at the same time less happy in their humour and less simple in their pathos. "What pleases *me* as simple and naive," says Burns to Thomson, "disgusts *you* as ludicrous and low. For this reason 'Fye, gie me my coggie, sirs,' 'Fye, let us a' to the bridal,' with several others of that cast, are to me highly pleasing, while 'Saw ye my Father' delights me with its descriptive simple pathos:" we read in these words the reasons of the difference between the lyrics of the two collections.

The land where the poet lived furnished ready materials for song: hills with fine woods, vales with clear waters, and dames as lovely as any recorded in verse, were to be had in his walks and his visits; while, for the purposes of mirth or of humour, characters, in whose faces originality was legibly written, were as numerous in Nithsdale as he had found them in the west. He had been reproached, while in Kyle, with seeing charms in very ordinary looks, and hanging the garlands of the muse on unlovely altars; he was liable to no such censure in Nithsdale; he poured out the incense of poetry only on the fair and captivating: his Jeans, his Lucys, his Phillises, and his Jessies were ladies of such mental or personal charms as the Reynolds's and the Lawrences of the time would have rejoiced to lay out their choicest colours on. But he did not limit himself to the charms of those whom he could step out to the walks and admire: his lyrics give evidence of the wandering of his thoughts to the distant or the dead — he loves to remember Charlotte Hamilton and Mary Campbell, and think of the sighs and vows on the Devon and the Doon, while his harpstrings were still quivering to the names of the Millers and the M'Murdos — to the charms of the lasses with golden or with flaxen locks, in the valley where he dwelt. Of Jean M'Murdo and her sister Phillis he loved to sing; and their beauty merited his strains: to one who died in her bloom, Lucy Johnston, he addressed a song of great sweetness; to Jessie Lewars, two or three songs of gratitude and praise: nor did he forget other beauties, for the accomplished Mrs. Riddel is remembered, and the absence of fair Clarinda is lamented in strains both impassioned and pathetic.

But the main inspirer of the latter songs of Burns was a young woman of humble birth: of a form equal to the most exquisite proportions of sculpture, with bloom on her cheeks, and merriment in her large bright eyes, enough to drive an amatory poet crazy. Her name was Jean Lorimer; she was not more than seventeen when the poet made her acquaintance, and though she had got a sort of brevet-right from an officer of the army, to use his southron name of Whelpdale, she loved best to be addressed by her maiden designation, while the poet chose to veil her in the numerous lyrics, to which she gave life, under the names of "Chloris," "The lass of Craigie-burnwood," and "The lassie wi' the lintwhite locks." Though of a temper not much inclined to conceal anything, Burns complied so tastefully with the growing demand of the age for the exterior decencies of life, that when the scrupling dames of Caledonia sung a new song in her praise, they were as unconscious whence its beauties came, as is the lover of art, that the shape and gracefulness of the marble nymph which he admires, are derived from a creature who sells the use of her charms indifferently to sculpture or to love. Fine poetry, like other arts called fine, springs from "strange places," as the flower in the fable said, when it bloomed on the dunghill; nor is Burns more to be blamed than was Raphael, who painted Madonnas, and Magdalens with dishevelled hair and lifted eyes, from a loose lady, whom the pope, "Holy at Rome — here Antichrist," charitably prescribed to the artist, while he laboured in the cause of the church. Of the poetic use which he made of Jean Lorimer's charms, Burns gives this account to Thomson. "The lady of whom the song of Craigie-burnwood was made is one of the finest women in Scotland, and in fact is to me in a manner what Sterne's Eliza was to him — a mistress, or friend, or what you will, in the guileless simplicity of platonic love. I assure you that to my lovely friend you are indebted for many of my best songs. Do you think that the sober gin-horse routine of my existence could inspire a man with life and love and joy — could fire him with enthusiasm, or melt him with pathos, equal to the genius of your book? No! no! Whenever I want to be more than ordinary in song — to be in

49

some degree equal to your diviner airs — do you imagine I fast and pray for the celestial emanation? Quite the contrary. I have a glorious recipe; the very one that for his own use was invented by the divinity of healing and poesy, when erst he piped to the flocks of Admetus. I put myself in a regimen of admiring a fine woman; and in proportion to the adorability of her charms, in proportion are you delighted with my verses. The lightning of her eye is the godhead of Parnassus, and the witchery of her smile, the divinity of Helicon."

Most of the songs which he composed under the influences to which I have alluded are of the first order: "Bonnie Lesley," "Highland Mary," "Auld Rob Morris," "Duncan Gray," "Wandering Willie," "Meg o' the Mill," "The poor and honest sodger," "Bonnie Jean," "Phillis the fair," "John Anderson my Jo," "Had I a cave on some wild distant shore," "Whistle and I'll come to you, my lad," "Bruce's Address to his men at Bannockburn," "Auld Lang Syne," "Thine am I, my faithful fair," "Wilt thou be my dearie," "O Chloris, mark how green the groves," "Contented wi' little, and cantie wi' mair," "Their groves of sweet myrtle," "Last May a braw wooer came down the long glen," "O Mally's meek, Mally's sweet," "Hey for a lass wi' a tocher," "Here's a health to ane I loe dear," and the "Fairest maid on Devon banks." Many of the latter lyrics of Burns were more or less altered, to put them into better harmony with the airs, and I am not the only one who has wondered that a bard so impetuous and intractable in most matters, should have become so soft and pliable, as to make changes which too often sacrificed the poetry for the sake of a fuller and more swelling sound. It is true that the emphatic notes of the music must find their echo in the emphatic words of the verse, and that words soft and liquid are fitter for ladies' lips, than words hissing and rough; but it is also true that in changing a harsher word for one more harmonious the sense often suffers, and that happiness of expression, and that dance of words which lyric verse requires, lose much of their life and vigour. The poet's favourite walk in composing his songs was on a beautiful green sward on the northern side of the Nith, opposite Lincluden: and his favourite posture for composition at home was balancing himself on the hind legs of his arm-chair.

While indulging in these lyrical nights, politics penetrated into Nithsdale, and disturbed the tranquillity of that secluded region. First, there came a contest far the representation of the Dumfries district of boroughs, between Patrick Miller, younger, of Dalswinton, and Sir James Johnstone, of Westerhall, and some two years afterwards, a struggle for the representation of the county of Kirkcudbright, between the interest of the

Stewarts, of Galloway, and Patrick Heron, of Kerroughtree. In the first of these the poet mingled discretion with his mirth, and raised a hearty laugh, in which both parties joined; for this sobriety of temper, good reasons may be assigned: Miller, the elder, of Dalswinton, had desired to oblige him in the affair of Ellisland, and his firm and considerate friend, M'Murdo, of Drumlanrig, was chamberlain to his Grace of Queensbury, on whoso interest Miller stood. On the other hand, his old Jacobitical affections made him the secret well-wisher to Westerhall, for up to this time, at least till acid disappointment and the democratic doctrine of the natural equality of man influenced him, Burns, or as a western rhymer of his day and district worded the reproach — Rob was a Tory. His situation, it will therefore be observed, disposed him to moderation, and accounts for the milkiness of his Epistle to Fintray, in which he marshals the chiefs of the contending factions, and foretells the fierceness of the strife, without pretending to foresee the event. Neither is he more explicit, though infinitely more humorous, in his ballad of "The Five Carlins," in which he impersonates the five boroughs — Dumfries, Kirkcudbright, Lochmaben, Sanquhar, and Annan, and draws their characters as shrewd and calculating dames, met in much wrath and drink to choose a representative.

But the two or three years which elapsed between the election for the boroughs, and that for the county adjoining, wrought a serious change in the temper as well as the opinions of the poet. His Jacobitism, as has been said was of a poetic kind, and put on but in obedience to old feelings, and made no part of the man: he was in his heart as democratic as the kirk of Scotland, which educated him — he acknowledged no other superiority but the mental: "he was disposed, too," said Professor Walker, "from constitutional temper, from education and the accidents of life, to a jealousy of power, and a keen hostility against every system which enabled birth and opulence to anticipate those rewards which he conceived to belong to genius and virtue." When we add to this, a resentment of the injurious treatment of the dispensers of public patronage, who had neglected his claims, and showered pensions and places on men unworthy of being named with him, we have assigned causes for the change of side and the tone of asperity and bitterness infused into "The Heron Ballads." Formerly honey was mixed with his gall: a little praise sweetened his censure: in these election lampoons he is fierce and even venomous:— no man has a head but what is empty, nor a heart that is not black: men descended without reproach from lines of heroes are stigmatized as cowards, and the honest and conscientious are reproached as miserly, mean, and dishonourable. Such is the spirit of party. "I have privately," thus writes the poet to Heron, "printed a good many copies of the ballads, and have sent them among friends about the country. You have already, as your auxiliary, the sober detestation of mankind on the heads of your opponents; find I swear by the lyre of Thalia, to muster on your side all the votaries of honest laughter and fair, candid ridicule." The ridicule was uncandid, and the laughter dishonest. The poet was unfortunate in his political attachments: Miller gained the boroughs which Burns wished he might lose, and Heron lost the county which he foretold he would gain. It must also be recorded against the good taste of the poet, that he loved to recite "The Heron Ballads," and reckon them among his happiest compositions.

From attacking others, the poet was — in the interval between penning these election lampoons — called on to defend himself: for this he seems to have been quite unprepared, though in those yeasty times he might have expected it. "I have been surprised, confounded, and distracted," he thus writes to Graham, of Fintray, "by Mr. Mitchell, the collector, telling me that he has received an order from your board to inquire into my political conduct, and blaming me as a person disaffected to government. Sir, you are a husband and a father: you know what you would feel, to see the much-loved wife of your bosom, and your helpless prattling little ones, turned adrift into the world, degraded and disgraced, from a situation in which they had been respectable and respected. I would not tell a deliberate falsehood, no, not though even worse horrors, if worse can be than those I have mentioned, hung over my head, and I say that the allegation, whatever villain has made it, is a lie! To the British constitution, on Revolution principles, next after my God, I am devotedly attached. To your patronage as a man of some genius, you have allowed me a claim; and your esteem as an honest man I know is my due. To these, sir, permit me to appeal: by these I adjure you to save me from that misery which threatens to overwhelm me, and which with my latest breath I will say I have not deserved." In this letter, another, intended for the eye of the Commissioners of the Board of Excise, was enclosed, in which he disclaimed entertaining the idea of a British republic — a wild dream of the day — but stood by the principles of the constitution of 1688, with the wish to see such corruptions as had crept in, amended. This last remark, it appears, by a letter from the poet to Captain Erskine, afterwards Earl of Mar, gave great offence, for Corbet, one of the superiors, was desired to inform him, "that his business was to act, and not to think; and that whatever might be men or measures, it was his duty to be silent and obedient." The intercession of Fintray, and the explanations of Burns, were so far effectual, that his political offense was forgiven, "only I understand," said he, "that all hopes of my getting officially forward are blasted." The records of the Excise Office exhibit no trace of this memorable matter, and two noblemen, who were then in the government, have assured me that this harsh proceeding received no countenance at head-quarters, and must have originated with some ungenerous or malicious person, on whom the poet had spilt a little of the nitric acid of his wrath.

That Burns was numbered among the republicans of Dumfries I well remember: but then those who held different sentiments from the men in power, were all, in that loyal town, stigmatized as democrats: that he either desired to see the constitution changed, or his country invaded by the liberal French, who proposed to set us free with the bayonet, and then admit us to the "fraternal embrace," no one ever believed. It is true that he spoke of premiers and peers with contempt; that he hesitated to take off his hat in the theatre, to the air of "God save the king;" that he refused to drink the health of Pitt, saying he preferred that of Washington — a far greater man; that he wrote bitter words against that combination of princes, who desired to put down freedom in France; that he said the titled spurred and the wealthy switched England and Scotland like two hack-horses; and that all the high places of the land, instead of being filled by genius and talent, were occupied, as were the high-places of Israel, with idols of wood or of stone. But all this and more had been done and said before by thousands in this land, whose love of their country was never questioned. That it was bad taste to refuse to remove his hat when other heads were bared, and little better to refuse to pledge in company the name of Pitt, because he preferred Washington, cannot admit of a doubt; but that he deserved to be written down traitor, for mere matters of whim or caprice, or to be turned out of the unenvied situation of "gauging auld wives' barrels," because he thought there were some stains on the white robe of the constitution, seems a sort of tyranny new in the history of oppression. His love of country is recorded in too many undying lines to admit of a doubt now: nor is it that chivalrous love alone which men call romantic; it is a love which may be laid up in every man's heart and practised in every man's life; the words are homely, but the words of Burns are always expressive:—

"The kettle of the kirk and state

Perhaps a clout may fail in't,

But deil a foreign tinkler loon

Shall ever ca' a nail in't.

Be Britons still to Britons true,

Amang ourselves united;

For never but by British hands

Shall British wrongs be righted."

But while verses, deserving as these do to become the national motto, and sentiments loyal and generous, were overlooked and forgotten, all his rash words about freedom, and his sarcastic sallies about thrones and kings, were treasured up to his injury, by the mean and the malicious. His steps were watched and his words weighed; when he talked with a friend in the street, he was supposed to utter sedition; and when ladies retired from the table, and the wine circulated with closed doors, he was suspected of treason rather than of toasting, which he often did with much humour, the charms of woman; even when he gave as a sentiment, "May our success be equal to the justice of our cause," he was liable to be challenged by some gunpowder captain, who thought that we deserved success in war, whether right or wrong. It is true that he hated with a most cordial hatred all who presumed on their own consequence, whether arising from wealth, titles, or commissions in the army; officers he usually called "the epauletted puppies," and lords he generally spoke of as "feather-headed fools," who could but strut and stare and be no answer in kind to retort his satiric flings, his unfriends reported that it was unsafe for young men to associate with one whose principles were democratic, and scarcely either modest or safe for young women to listen to a poet whose notions of female virtue were so loose and his songs so free. These sentiments prevailed so far that a gentleman on a visit from London, told me he was dissuaded from inviting Burns to a dinner, given by way of welcome back to his native place, because he was the associate of democrats and loose people; and when a modest dame of Dumfries expressed, through a friend, a wish to have but the honour of speaking to one of whose genius she was an admirer, the poet declined the interview, with a half-serious smile, saying, "Alas! she is handsome, and you know the character publicly assigned to me." She escaped the danger of being numbered, it is likely, with the Annas and the Chlorises of his freer strains.

The neglect of his country, the tyranny of the Excise, and the downfall of his hopes and fortunes, were now to bring forth their fruits — the poet's health began to decline. His drooping looks, his neglect of his person, his solitary saunterings, his escape from the stings of reflection into socialities, and his distempered joy in the company of beauty, all spoke, as plainly as with a tongue, of a sinking heart and a declining body. Yet though he was sensible of sinking health, hope did not at once desert him: he continued to pour out such tender strains, and to show such flashes of wit and humour at the call of Thomson, as are recorded of no other lyrist: neither did he, when in company after his own mind, hang the head, and speak mournfully, but talked and smiled and still charmed all listeners by his witty vivacities.

On the 20th of June, 1795, he writes thus of his fortunes and condition to his friend Clarke, "Still, still the victim of affliction; were you to see the emaciated figure who now holds the pen to you, you would not know your old friend. Whether I shall ever get about again is only known to HIM, the Great Unknown, whoso creature I am. Alas, Clarke, I begin to fear the worst! As to my individual self I am tranquil, and would despise myself if I were not: but Burns's poor widow and half-a-dozen of his dear little ones, helpless orphans! *Here* I am as weak as a woman's tear. Enough of this! 'tis half my disease. I duly received your last, enclosing the note: it came extremely in time, and I am much obliged to your punctuality. Again I must request you to do me the same kindness. Be so very good as by return of post to enclose me *another* note: I trust you can do so without inconvenience, and it will seriously oblige me. If I must go, I leave a few friends behind me, whom I shall regret while consciousness remains. I know I shall live in their remembrance. O, dear, dear Clarke! that I shall ever see you again is I am afraid highly improbable." This remarkable letter proves both the declining health, and the poverty of the poet: his digestion was so bad that he could taste neither flesh nor fish: porridge and milk he could alone swallow, and that but in small quantities. When it is recollected that he had no more than thirty shillings a week to keep house, and live like a gentleman, no one need wonder that his wife had to be obliged to a generous neighbour for some of the chief necessaries for her coming confinement, and that the poet had to beg, in extreme need, two guinea notes from a distant friend.

His sinking state was not unobserved by his friends, and Syme and M'Murdo united with Dr. Maxwell in persuading him, at the beginning of the summer, to seek health at the Brow-well, a few miles east of Dumfries, where there were pleasant walks on the Solway-side, and salubrious breezes from the sea, which it was expected would bring the health to the poet they had brought to many. For a while, his looks brightened up, and health seemed inclined to return: his friend, the witty and accomplished Mrs. Riddel, who was herself ailing, paid him a visit. "I was struck," she said, "with his appearance on entering the room: the stamp of death was impressed on his features. His first words were, 'Well, Madam, have you any commands for the other world?' I replied that it seemed a doubtful case which of us should be there soonest; he looked in my face with an air of great kindness, and expressed his concern at seeing me so ill, with his usual sensibility. At table he ate little or nothing: we had a long conversation about his present state, and the approaching termination of all his earthly prospects. He showed great concern about his literary fame, and particularly the publication of his posthumous works; he said he was well aware that his death would occasion some noise, and that every scrap of his writing would be revived against him, to the injury of his future reputation; that letters and verses, written with unguarded freedom, would be handed about by vanity or malevolence when no dread of his resentment would restrain them, or prevent malice or envy from pouring forth their venom on his name. I had seldom seen his mind greater, or more collected. There was frequently a considerable degree of vivacity in his sallies; but the concern and dejection I could not disguise, damped the spirit of pleasantry he seemed willing to indulge." This was on the evening of the 5th of July; another lady who called to see him, found him seated at a window, gazing on the sun, then setting brightly on the summits of the green hills of Nithsdale. "Look how lovely the sun is," said the poet, "but he will soon have done with shining for me."

He now longed for home: his wife, whom he ever tenderly loved, was about to be confined in child-bed: his papers were in sad confusion, and required arrangement; and he felt that desire to die, at least, among familiar things and friendly faces, so common to our nature. He had not long before, though much reduced in pocket, refused with scorn an offer of fifty pounds, which a speculating bookseller made, for leave to publish his looser compositions; he had refused an offer of the like sum yearly, from Perry of the Morning Chronicle, for poetic contributions to his paper, lest it might embroil him with the ruling powers, and he had resented the remittance of five pounds from Thomson, on account of his lyric contributions, and desired him to do so no more, unless he wished to quarrel with him; but his necessities now, and they had at no time been so great, induced him to solicit five pounds from Thomson, and ten pounds from his cousin, James Burness, of Montrose, and to beg his friend Alexander Cunningham to intercede with the Commissioners of Excise, to depart from their usual practice, and grant him his full salary; "for without that," he added, "if I die not of disease, I must perish with hunger." Thomson sent the five pounds, James Burness sent the ten, but the Commissioners of Excise refused to be either merciful or generous. Stobie, a young expectant in the customs, was both; — he performed the duties of the dying poet, and refused to touch the salary. The mind of Burns was haunted with the fears of want and the terrors of a jail; nor were those fears without foundation; one Williamson, to whom he was indebted for the cloth to make his volunteer regimentals, threatened the one; and a feeling that he was without money for either his own illness or the confinement of his wife, threatened the other.

Burns returned from the Brow-well, on the 18th of July: as he walked from the little carriage which brought him up the Mill hole-brae to his own door, he trembled much, and stooped with weakness and pain, and kept his feet with difficulty: his looks were woe-worn and ghastly, and no one who saw him, and there were several, expected to see him again in life. It was soon circulated through Dumfries, that Burns had returned worse from the Brow-well; that Maxwell thought ill of him, and that, in truth, he was dying. The anxiety of all classes was great; differences of opinion were forgotten, in sympathy for his early fate: wherever two or three were met together their talk was of Burns, of his rare wit, matchless humour, the vivacity of his conversation, and the kindness of his heart. To the poet himself, death, which he now knew was at hand, brought with it no fear; his good-humour, which small matters alone ruffled, did not forsake him, and his wit was ever ready. He was poor — he gave his pistols, which he had used against the smugglers on the Solway, to his physician, adding with a smile, that he had tried them and found them an honour to their maker, which was more than he could say of the bulk of mankind! He was proud — he remembered the indifferent practice of the corps to which he belonged, and turning to Gibson, one of his fellow-soldiers, who stood at his bedside with wet eyes, "John," said he, and a gleam of humour passed over his face, "pray don't let the awkward-squad fire over me." It was almost the last act of his life to copy into his Common-place Book, the letters which contained the charge against him of the Commissioners of Excise, and his own eloquent refutation, leaving judgment to be pronounced by the candour of posterity.

It has been injuriously said of Burns, by Coleridge, that the man sunk, but the poet was bright to the last: he did not sink in the sense that these words imply: the man was manly to the latest draught of breath. That he was a poet to the last, can be proved by facts, as well as by the word of the author of Christabel. As he lay silently growing weaker and weaker, he observed Jessie Lewars, a modest and beautiful young creature, and sister to one of his brethren of the Excise, watching over him with moist eyes, and tending him with the care of a daughter; he rewarded her with one of those songs which are an insurance against forgetfulness. The lyrics of the north have nothing finer than this exquisite stanza:—

"Altho' thou maun never be mine,

Altho' even hope is denied,

'Tis sweeter for thee despairing,

Than aught in the world beside."

His thoughts as he lay wandered to Charlotte Hamilton, and he dedicated some beautiful stanzas to her beauty and her coldness, beginning, "Fairest maid on Devon banks."

It was a sad sight to see the poet gradually sinking; his wife in hourly expectation of her sixth confinement, and his four helpless children — a daughter, a sweet child, had died the year before — with no one of their lineage to soothe them with kind words or minister to their wants. Jessie Lewars, with equal prudence and attention, watched over them all: she could not help seeing that the thoughts of the desolation which his death would bring, pressed sorely on him, for he loved his children, and hoped much from his boys. He wrote to his father-in-law, James Armour, at Mauchline, that he was dying, his wife nigh her confinement, and begged that his mother-in-law would hasten to them and speak comfort. He wrote to Mrs. Dunlop, saying, "I have written to you so often without receiving any answer that I would not trouble you again, but for the circumstances in which I am. An illness which has long hung about me in all probability will speedily send me beyond that bourne whence no traveller returns. Your friendship, with which for many years you honoured me, was a friendship dearest to my soul: your conversation and your correspondence were at once highly entertaining and instructive — with what pleasure did I use to break up the seal! The remembrance yet adds one pulse more to my poor palpitating heart. Farewell!" A tremor pervaded his frame; his tongue grew parched, and he was at times delirious: on the fourth day after his return, when his attendant, James Maclure, held his medicine to his lips, he swallowed it eagerly, rose almost wholly up, spread out his hands, sprang forward nigh the whole length of the bed, fell on his face, and expired. He died on the 21st of July, when nearly thirty-seven years and seven months old.

The burial of Burns, on the 25th of July, was an impressive and mournful scene: half the people of Nithsdale and the neighbouring parts of Galloway had crowded into Dumfries, to see their poet "mingled with the earth," and not a few had been permitted to look at his body, laid out for interment. It was a calm and beautiful day, and as the body was borne along the street towards the old kirk-yard, by his brethren of the volunteers, not a sound was heard but the measured step and the solemn music: there was no impatient crushing, no fierce elbowing — the crowd which filled the street seemed conscious of what they were now losing for ever. Even while this pageant was passing, the widow of the poet was taken in labour; but the infant born in that unhappy hour soon shared his father's grave. On reaching the northern nook of the kirk-yard, where the grave was made, the mourners halted; the coffin was divested of the mort-cloth, and silently lowered to its resting-place, and as the first shovel-full of earth fell on the lid, the volunteers, too agitated to be steady, justified the fears of the poet, by three ragged volleys. He who now writes this very brief and imperfect account, was present: he thought then, as he thinks now, that all the military array of foot and horse did not harmonize with either the genius or the fortunes of the poet, and that the tears which he saw on many cheeks around, as the earth was replaced, were worth all the splendour of a show which mocked with unintended mockery the burial of the poor and neglected Burns. The body of the poet was, on the 5th of June, 1815, removed to a more commodious spot in the same burial-ground — his dark, and waving locks looked then fresh and glossy — to afford room for a marble monument, which embodies, with neither skill nor grace, that well-known passage in the dedication to the gentlemen of the Caledonian Hunt:—"The poetic genius of my country found me, as the prophetic bard, Elijah, did Elisha, at the plough, and threw her inspiring mantle over me." The dust of the bard was again disturbed, when the body of Mrs. Burns was laid, in April, 1834, beside the remains of her husband: his skull was dug up by the district craniologists, to satisfy their minds by measurement that he was equal to the composition of "Tam o' Shanter," or "Mary in Heaven." This done, they placed the skull in a leaden box, "carefully lined with the softest materials," and returned it, we hope for ever, to the hallowed ground.

Thus lived and died Robert Burns, the chief of Scottish poets: in his person he was tall and sinewy, and of such strength and activity, that Scott alone, of all the poets I have seen, seemed his equal: his forehead was broad, his hair black, with an inclination to curl, his visage uncommonly swarthy, his eyes large, dark and lustrous, and his voice deep and manly. His sensibility was strong, his passions full to overflowing, and he loved,

59

nay, adored, whatever was gentle and beautiful. He had, when a lad at the plough, an eloquent word and an inspired song for every fair face that smiled on him, and a sharp sarcasm or a fierce lampoon for every rustic who thwarted or contradicted him. As his first inspiration came from love, he continued through life to love on, and was as ready with the lasting incense of the muse for the ladies of Nithsdale as for the lasses of Kyle: his earliest song was in praise of a young girl who reaped by his side, when he was seventeen — his latest in honour of a lady by whose side he had wandered and dreamed on the banks of the Devon. He was of a nature proud and suspicious, and towards the close of his life seemed disposed to regard all above him in rank as men who unworthily possessed the patrimony of genius: he desired to see the order of nature restored, and worth and talent in precedence of the base or the dull. He had no medium in his hatred or his love; he never spared the stupid, as if they were not to be endured because he was bright; and on the heads of the innocent possessors of titles or wealth he was ever ready to shower his lampoons. He loved to start doubts in religion which he knew inspiration only could solve, and he spoke of Calvinism with a latitude of language that grieved pious listeners. He was warm-hearted and generous to a degree, above all men, and scorned all that was selfish and mean with a scorn quite romantic. He was a steadfast friend and a good neighbour: while he lived at Ellisland few passed his door without being entertained at his table; and even when in poverty, on the Millhole-brae, the poor seldom left his door but with blessings on their lips.

Of his modes of study he has himself informed us, as well as of the seasons and the places in which he loved to muse. He composed while he strolled along the secluded banks of the Doon, the Ayr, or the Nith: as the images crowded on his fancy his pace became quickened, and in his highest moods he was excited even to tears. He loved the winter for its leafless trees, its swelling floods, and its winds which swept along the gloomy sky, with frost and snow on their wings: but he loved the autumn more — he has neglected to say why — the muse was then more liberal of her favours, and he composed with a happy alacrity unfelt in all other seasons. He filled his mind and heart with the materials of song — and retired from gazing on woman's beauty, and from the excitement of her charms, to record his impressions in verse, as a painter delineates oil his canvas the looks of those who sit to his pencil. His chief place of study at Ellisland is still remembered: it extends along the river-bank towards the Isle: there the neighbouring gentry love to walk and peasants to gather, and hold it sacred, as the place where he composed Tam O' Shanter. His favourite place of study when residing in Dumfries, was the ruins of Lincluden

College, made classic by that sublime ode, "The Vision," and that level and clovery sward contiguous to the College, on the northern side of the Nith: the latter place was his favourite resort; it is known now by the name of Burns's musing ground, and there he conceived many of his latter lyrics. In case of interruption he completed the verses at the fireside, where he swung to and fro in his arm-chair till the task was done: he then submitted the song to the ordeal of his wife's voice, which was both sweet and clear, and while she sung he listened attentively, and altered or amended till the whole was in harmony, music and words.

The genius of Burns is of a high order: in brightness of expression and unsolicited ease and natural vehemence of language, he stands in the first rank of poets: in choice of subjects, in happiness of conception, and loftiness of imagination, he recedes into the second. He owes little of his fame to his objects, for, saving the beauty of a few ladies, they were all of an ordinary kind: he sought neither in romance nor in history for themes to the muse; he took up topics from life around which were familiar to all, and endowed them with character, with passion, with tenderness, with humour — elevating all that he touched into the regions of poetry and morals. He went to no far lands for the purpose of surprising us with wonders, neither did he go to crowns or coronets to attract the stare of the peasantry around him, by things which to them were as a book shut and sealed: "The Daisy" grew on the lands which he ploughed; "The Mouse" built her frail nest on his own stubble-field; "The Haggis" reeked on his own table; "The Scotch Drink" of which he sang was the produce of a neighbouring still; "The Twa Dogs," which conversed so wisely and wittily, were, one of them at least, his own collies; "The Vision" is but a picture, and a brilliant one, of his own hopes and fears; "Tam Samson" was a friend whom he loved; "Doctor Hornbook" a neighbouring pedant; "Matthew Henderson" a social captain on half-pay; "The Scotch Bard" who had gone to the West Indies was Burns himself; the heroine of "The Lament," was Jean Armour; and "Tam O' Shanter" a facetious farmer of Kyle, who rode late and loved pleasant company, nay, even "The Deil" himself, whom he had the hardihood to address, was a being whose eldrich croon bad alarmed the devout matrons of Kyle, and had wandered, not unseen by the bard himself, among the lonely glens of the Doon. Burns was one of the first to teach the world that high moral poetry resided in the humblest subjects: whatever he touched became elevated; his spirit possessed and inspired the commonest topics, and endowed them with life and beauty.

His songs have all the beauties and but few of them the faults of his poems: they flow to the music as readily as if both air and words came into the world together. The sentiments are from nature, they are rarely strained or forced, and the words dance in their places and echo the music in its pastoral sweetness, social glee, or in the tender and the moving. He seems always to write with woman's eye upon him: he is gentle, persuasive and impassioned: he appears to watch her looks, and pours out his praise or his complaint according to the changeful moods of her mind. He looks on her, too, with a sculptor's as well as a poet's eye: to him who works in marble, the diamonds, emeralds, pearls, and elaborate ornaments of gold, but load and injure the harmony of proportion, the grace of form, and divinity of sentiment of his nymph or his goddess — so with Burns the fashion of a lady's boddice, the lustre of her satins, or the sparkle of her diamonds, or other finery with which wealth or taste has loaded her, are neglected us idle frippery; while her beauty, her form, or her mind, matters which are of nature and not of fashion, are remembered and praised. He is none of the millinery bards, who deal in scented silks, spider-net laces, rare gems, set in rarer workmanship, and who shower diamonds and pearls by the bushel on a lady's locks: he makes bright eyes, flushing cheeks, the magic of the tongue, and the "pulses' maddening play" perform all. His songs are, in general, pastoral pictures: he seldom finishes a portrait of female beauty without enclosing it in a natural frame-work of waving woods, running streams, the melody of birds, and the lights of heaven. Those who desire to feel Burns in all his force, must seek some summer glen, when a country girl searches among his many songs for one which sympathizes with her own heart, and gives it full utterance, till wood and vale is filled with the melody. It is remarkable that the most naturally elegant and truly impassioned songs in our literature were written by a ploughman in honour of the rustic lasses around him.

His poetry is all life and energy, and bears the impress of a warm heart and a clear understanding: it abounds with passions and opinions — vivid pictures of rural happiness and the raptures of successful love, all fresh from nature and observation, and not as they are seen through the spectacles of books. The wit of the clouted shoe is there without its coarseness: there is a prodigality of humour without licentiousness, a pathos ever natural and manly, a social joy akin sometimes to sadness, a melancholy not unallied to mirth, and a sublime morality which seeks to elevate and soothe. To a love of man he added an affection for the flowers of the valley, the fowls of the air, and the beasts of the field: he perceived the tie of social sympathy which united animated with unanimated nature, and in many of his finest poems most beautifully he has enforced it. His thoughts are original and his style new and unborrowed: all that he has written is distinguished by a happy carelessness, a bounding elasticity of spirit, and a singular felicity of expression, simple yet inimitable; he is familiar yet dignified, careless, yet correct, and concise, yet clear and full. All this and much more is embodied in the language of humble life — a dialect reckoned barbarous by scholars, but which, coming from the lips of inspiration, becomes classic and elevated.

The prose of this great poet has much of the original merit of his verse, but it is seldom so natural and so sustained: it abounds with fine outflashings and with a genial warmth and vigour, but it is defaced by false ornament and by a constant anxiety to say fine and forcible things. He seems not to know that simplicity was as rare and as needful a beauty in prose as in verse; he covets the pauses of Sterne and the point and antithesis of Junius, like one who believes that to write prose well he must be ever lively, ever pointed, and ever smart. Yet the account which he wrote of himself to Dr. Moore is one of the most spirited and natural narratives in the language, and composed in a style remote from the strained and groped-for witticisms and put-on sensibilities of many of his letters:— "Simple," as John Wilson says, "we may well call it; rich in fancy, overflowing in feeling, and dashed off in every other paragraph with the easy boldness of a great master."

Made in the USA
San Bernardino, CA
11 July 2018